BEYOND CHARITY

10 YEARS OF OXFAM INDIA

SAVVY SOUMYA MISRA

BLOOMSBURY
NEW DELHI • LONDON • OXFORD • NEW YORK • SYDNEY

BLOOMSBURY INDIA
Bloomsbury Publishing India Pvt. Ltd
Second Floor, LSC Building No. 4, DDA Complex, Pocket C – 6 & 7,
Vasant Kunj New Delhi 110070

BLOOMSBURY, BLOOMSBURY PRIME and the Diana logo are trademarks of Bloomsbury Publishing Plc

First published 2019

ISBN: 978-93-89391-98-5

2 4 6 8 10 9 7 5 3 1

Printed and bound in India by Replika Press Pvt Ltd

Dedicated to
each and everyone who
worked at Oxfam to
build its rich legacy
in India

Contents

Acknowledgements

Beyond Charity: 10 Years of Oxfam India wouldn't be possible without all the people who made these stories come to life—those who worked at Oxfam, those who worked with the partner and grassroots organisations and those who funded these projects.

I am grateful to every partner NGO and individual we worked with in the last 10 years, and before that, for making these stories possible. Though not everyone has been written about in the book, and it was a difficult choice to make, it does not take away the brilliant contributions made by each one of them. This book also wouldn't be possible without the communities who accepted Oxfam with open arms and became co-travellers, integral to this journey of bringing about a change.

I would like to thank Nisha Agrawal, former CEO of Oxfam India, for believing in the idea of this book and showing the faith and confidence in me to go through with the plan. Her contribution at every stage of the book has been immense and extremely important.

A special shout out to Ranjana Das, a colleague and a very dear friend, for being my sounding board, for ideating with me, for being the go-to person for all and any information on the history of Oxfam India. If she did not have the information, she knew who would!

Many thanks to Avinash Kumar, former director at Oxfam India (and now with Water Aid), for entertaining my book idea, walking me through the history of Oxfam and feeding me lunch. Thanks to Amitabh Behar, our current CEO, for taking out the time to talk of his experience with Oxfam in the past.

Special thanks to my current boss Tejas Patel for constantly motivating me to write and making sure the book was completed. In the last one month, he had become, what I call, a 'slave-driver'.

Thanks to my colleague Himanshi Matta for coming up with the title of the book.

Thanks to Lucy Dubochet, Pooja Parvati, Diya Dutta, Ranu Kayastha Bhogal and Rina Soni—the bosses I had over the last five years—for giving me the opportunity at Oxfam and for letting me be!

I am grateful to each and everyone I met during the course of researching for the book. The fact that all of them agreed to meet even when many of these projects were over, for many years now, spoke volume of Oxfam's legacy. And meeting with people who made these projects happen, reinstated my faith in the idea that these stories needed to be told.

I would take this opportunity to thank them individually (and apologies in advance if I have missed out anyone)—Vijay Kumar 'Babloo' (formerly PGVS); Rehana Adib and her team (Astitva); Raju Narzary (NERSWM) and his team; Neelam

Prabhat (Aaroh Campaign); Dr Shiraz A Wajih (GEAG); Bharat Bhushan (PANI); Govind Kelkar; Mangaraj Panda (UAA); Hugh and Sandra Davidson; Lingaiah (CROPS); Hepsibah (SYO); Murali, Ramamurthy and Jayarama Rao (MARI); Kaviraj (PSS); Dr Narasimha Reddy Donthi; Ramana Rao; T Yadagiri; Sanjay, Rajesh Kumar and Priya Bharti (Lokmitra); Devendra Gandhi (Samarth); Anil Pradhan (Sikshasandhan); Jameela Nishat and her team (Shaheen Resource Centre); K Satyavati (Bhumika Women's Collective); Sivakumari (SWARD); Chinmayee Joshi aka Sejal Ben (formerly AWAG), Jahnavi Andharia, Jeevika Shiv and Seema Joshi (ANANDI); Pushpanjali and Bhanu (ISWO); Danish Meeraj (BVHA); Dr Narendra Gupta (Prayas); Ganga Bhai (Chaupal); Ajay Bhagat (ASHA); HI Fatmi (SPARK); Manohar Kumar (Jan Sarokar); Rupesh ji and Ritwij (Koshish); Tushar Dash (Vasundhara); Francesco Obino.

I am very grateful to all ex-Oxfamers—Kanchan Sinha, Ashvin Dayal, Biranchi Upadhyay, Paromita Chowdhury, Kiran Nanavati, Amit Vatsyayan, Nishant Pandey, Sudha Rani Mullapudi, Girija D Boddupalli, Dhananjay Kakde, Mona Mehta, Sabita Parida, Anjali Bhardwaj, Pallavi Gupta, Abinash Lakhar, Rebecca David, Sanjeeta Gawri, Vanita Suneja, Farrukh Rahman Khan, Amita Pitre and Mary Thomas—who took time out from their busy schedule and shared valuable anecdotes, information and insights into the programmes and projects.

Thanks to those still around at Oxfam—Zubin Zaman, Deepak L Xavier, Bhaswar Banerjee, Santanu Dam, Shambhu

Nath Shaw, Vinuthna Patibandla, Mohan Parmar, Andrio Naskar, Anjela RV Taneja, Nand Kishore Singh, Akshaya Biswal, Anand Shukla, Binod Sinha, Pratiush Prakash, Prakash Gardia, Vijendra Aznabi, Sharmistha Bose—for ensuring the robustness of facts and incidents.

I am grateful to my very dear friends—Jasmeeta Dubey (Amma) and Indrajit Bose (Bose Man), for reading the drafts of my chapters and telling me they wanted to read the book; Sweta Dutta (Soy) and Nilanjana Ghosh Choudhury (Mashi) for being proud of me.

Thanks to my parents and brother for asking about the book, for pushing me to do better and to 'keep it up'.

Special thanks for my friend for life Udit Misra for being my back up, and my cook.

Let a Thousand Flowers Bloom

In 1997–98, Oxfam's Lucknow office got a visitor's request from Oxford. World-renowned philosopher, Philippa Foot, wanted to visit Oxfam's work in India; she wanted to see how women had changed over the years. She was nearly 80 years old. She visited the office and later that evening attended a dinner that the Lucknow office had hosted for her. "During the day when she visited our office, there was a grin on her face. I didn't ask her then but I did at dinner. 'You had a grin on your face at the office. What is it?'" Kanchan Sinha recounts. She headed Oxfam's (which was Oxfam Great Britain (OGB)) North India office in Lucknow, back then.

Philippa had replied that when she saw the office in Lucknow she was reminded of the Oxfam office in the 1940s. She had said, "We didn't have a table or chair. We were working out of classrooms of colleges at Oxford. Back then, we would have never imagined that a remote office of ours could ever have this kind of infrastructure."

Philippa was one of the earliest Oxfamers. She had joined the Oxford Committee for Famine Relief in 1948, as a student. Having remained involved with Oxfam throughout her life, she passed away in 2010. Philippa was visiting Oxfam in 1997–98. The organisation had come to India in 1951!

Oxfam was born out of a humanitarian crisis. It started as the Oxford Committee for Famine Relief in 1942. The committee was formed in response to the famine in Greece, as an aftermath of World War II, where nearly 2,00,000 Greeks died of starvation in the winter of 1941–42. The first time it came to India was also to respond to a humanitarian crisis. It was the Bihar famine of 1951. A grand total of £83,556 was sent as aid (money £16,711; clothing and supplies £66,845). This response won them appreciation in the House of Commons.[1]

Oxfam subsequently went on to provide emergency relief on several occasions of famine and drought in Bihar and parts of Western India; in 1971, it recruited 250 young doctors and medical students on the Indian side to attend to the Bengal refugees fleeing from the civil war in erstwhile East Pakistan (which later became Bangladesh). In 1960, Oxfam aligned with the Food and Agriculture Organisation's (FAO) Freedom from Hunger Campaign, which urged for immediate action on food shortage, and subsequently hunger, to beat the cycle of poverty. Under this project, Oxfam funded four international projects—the biggest was the grant for a feed compounding plant to Anand District Milk Producers' Cooperative (Amul).

Oxfam gave grants for relief work but the Oxfam Gramdan Action Programme (OGAP) changed it. As countries were gaining independence, Oxfam started focusing on development issues across the world. OGAP was initiated in 1966 by the

[1] Black, Maggie, ed. *A Cause for Our Times: Oxfam – the First 50 Years*. Oxfam, 1992.

then field director, Jim Howard, to tackle the famine situation in Bihar. Under the programme, wells were dug at the demand of the villagers; they provided the labour and Oxfam paid them with food. This was the first instance when Oxfam started working in partnership with a local NGO; this was also the first time they were working on an agricultural development programme and the first time they were working with a group of volunteers.

In the 1970s and 1980s, India was emerging out of Emergency and had a very dynamic social action movement. The changing political scenario paved the way for Oxfam to support grassroots organisations and individuals across the country in their cause for social development, and help them grow. Oxfam became popular among grassroots activists and civil society and it continues to be so today.

"There were several NGOs and individuals working at the grassroots. The concept was 'Let a Thousand Flowers Bloom'. OGB hence had the largest presence. It was present everywhere, barring Jammu and Kashmir and the North East. So people remember them," Ashvin Dayal explains the popularity of OGB. Ashvin worked with Oxfam for nearly 15 years; for the last 10 years, he has been with the Rockefeller Foundation.

In fact in the later years, when other affiliates like Oxfam Novib (Netherland), Oxfam Hong Kong, Oxfam Australia and Oxfam Intermon (Spain) also had their programmes across the country, OGB continued to have the largest presence.

Oxfam worked on a whole variety of themes—livelihood, agriculture, education, supply chain, health, gender-based violence, forest, mines, urban poverty, peacebuilding, humanitarian and, of course, droughts and famines. They worked with a whole range of individuals, grassroots organisations, larger organisations and networks. Kanchan recalls a campaign, in the 1990s, on ending violence against women in 16 districts of Bundelkhand—*Hinsa Sehna Band* (HISAB). "This was a campaign by women's organisations. And similar to a We Can Campaign but much before its time."

As mentioned above, OGB wasn't the only one that was funding projects in India. In the 1980s and 1990s, there were others such as Oxfam Hong Kong, Oxfam Novib (Netherlands), Oxfam Australia and Oxfam Intermon (Spain). Novib was the affiliate with the big money, they worked through consultants and supported the larger organisations; OGB did not have much money but had a very vast outreach working with smaller grassroots organisations; others were operating mostly in Western India or the northern state of Uttarakhand.

Globally, as Oxfam grew and spread to different countries, their offices began asserting a separate identity. Canada and the United States were the ones who started the trend. Hong Kong grew and became an independent affiliate in the late 1980s, as did New Zealand.

Though Oxfam India (OIN) became an independent affiliate in 2008, discussions on its autonomy had come up at several points in the 1970s and 1980s.

In her book, *A Cause of Our Times: Oxfam – the First 50 Years*, Maggie Black writes, "In India, a different impulse—that of decolonisation—is prompting discussions on whether the staff of the various Oxfams represented there should form their own 'Oxfam', raise their own funds, and gradually negotiate independence from the parent body. This is the first occasion on which the Oxfam policy of encouraging the growth of indigenous organisations and enabling them to build up capacity has led in this, quite logical, direction. A primarily recipient as opposed to donor Oxfam would be a new creation, and the practicalities have yet to be fully explored."

"Several reasons were given for these. Some saw it as a fundraising opportunity. Some thought that as a local organisation we could do more advocacy. Oxfam was being seen as a northern construct and there was a need for southern voice," says Ashvin.

In the meantime, Oxfam International (OI) was formed. This became the umbrella organisation. OI took over the role from OGB and the other affiliates that existed were harmonised.

By the turn of the millennium, India became a strong southern voice globally. "There was the question of the legitimacy of Oxfam International which called itself a global organisation but only with northern members. If it claimed that it was working in 100 countries to elevate the voices of the poor, it had to also work towards including these very voices in their own organisation," says Nisha Agrawal, the first CEO of Oxfam India (OIN).

There were other reasons too. Nisha continues, "In order to tap into the middle-income countries, which were the growth centres of the future, Oxfam wouldn't be able to raise fund as donors. There was a need to become an independent Indian NGO (while being a part of the larger international confederation of Oxfams) and involve more Indians in our work through fundraising."

This was also important considering that civil society space was getting constrained and foreign funds weren't looked at very kindly. This would eventually affect the policy advocacy space. As times were changing, there was a need for rights-based advocacy. An independent Indian NGO would make for easy access and acceptability among the policymakers.

Nisha further adds that there were members of the Indian civil society who had worked with Oxfam in the past and wanted an Indian Oxfam, "They wanted a large NGO that could play a part of a convener, a network and an alliance builder, and work as part of the Indian civil society."

All things considered, Oxfam India had very valid reasons to back its demand for becoming an independent affiliate—an autonomous body, with an Indian board and Indian CEO. Nisha Agrawal was the first CEO of Oxfam India. She joined in March 2008; OIN became an independent affiliate on 1 September 2008. Like the Oxford Committee for Famine Relief, Oxfam India too began with a humanitarian crisis; Oxfam first came to India to respond to Bihar famines, similarly, Oxfam India became an independent affiliate during the Kosi flood of August 2008, which was one of the worst floods in the history of the state.

This book marks the beginning of a journey for Oxfam and all the other international NGOs that were looking for legitimacy in a much more globally connected world. Within Oxfam, southern voices like Brazil, Mexico, China, Turkey, South Africa and India became prominent.

As we complete a decade in India, we take a pause to see if this model has delivered—whether we were able to do rights-based advocacy, build networks and alliances, raise funds and become a part of the Indian civil society. Oxfam India had a legacy of almost 57 years but when it started the journey as an independent affiliate, it was then at liberty to start off with a clean slate. This meant it could decide which states to work in and what projects to work on.

First up, it took stock of the states where it was needed the most. It turned its focus from the southern states to seven states in North and Eastern India that were socially and economically backward and were at the bottom of the table on practically all parameters. These states were Uttar Pradesh, Uttarakhand, Assam, Bihar, Chhattisgarh, Odisha and Jharkhand. Later, it pulled out of Uttarakhand.

Though the focus shifted from the south and west to the north and east, there remained continuity in the theme of work—Economic Justice (natural resource management),

Essential Services (education and health), Gender Justice (ending violence against women) and Humanitarian. What changed was the location and nature of the work.

The book has tried to capture the journey of the first 10 years of Oxfam India. Did it tick the boxes on the checklist it started with? How did it fare on the ones that it added as it went along?

Humanitarian work was the crowning glory of Oxfam and the newborn was put to test almost instantly. Oxfam India responded to the Kosi floods and much faster than it had done in the past. The Kosi response and recovery was a huge success (*When Kosi Flooded Supaul*). We inherited a strong legacy and an efficient team. But more than that, there was the freedom to, so to speak, Indianise the response—tailor-make it to suit the people who were affected and in need of help and support. Not only did Oxfam India run with the programme, it went beyond the six focus states. A fair amount of the humanitarian funds is raised within India.

Response to conflicts in Assam and Muzaffarnagar (*A Tale of Two Conflicts*), however, was a first of its kind. While the former was resource-based, the latter was communal. A foreign NGO would have hesitated but Oxfam India felt the need to respond. And it gave its best.

Like the humanitarian work, Oxfam India inherited the livelihood projects as well—the Cotton Textile Supply Chain (*For a Decent Living*) and Samudram fisheries project

(*Samudram Maadi*). These projects brought women and men together on a common platform and ensured that they earned a sustainable, decent living. Though they showed excellent results, these livelihood projects weren't pursued further because they lacked the component of rights-based advocacy, something that Oxfam India was building itself on.

Though these projects started before 2008, they continued even after Oxfam India was formed and left an indelible impression on the communities, the partner NGOs that were associated with it and Oxfam India's future projects as well. For instance, the strand of work with the garment factory workers in the cotton textile project laid the foundation for private sector engagement work on business and human rights at workplaces. Oxfam India stepped back from the fisheries project when it was on a high—the fisherwomen had become entrepreneurs and won international accolades for their work.

The key to rights-based advocacy was its fight to end violence against women (*To End Violence Against Women*) and the implementation of the Forest Rights Act (*Jal, Jangal, Zameen*). For the former, Oxfam India helped build institutions that women facing domestic violence could go to. It ran campaigns, and formed alliances and networks to push for the proper implementation of the Protection of Women from Domestic Violence Act, 2005 (PWDVA). In fact, it was able to advocate with Gujarat and Andhra Pradesh to institutionalise women support centres.

For the Forest Rights Act, Oxfam India went into Chhattisgarh at a time when many were leaving because of the conflict. Not only did it figure out a way to work in Chhattisgarh, it also formed a national network—Community Forest Rights-Learning and Advocacy (CFR-LA)—to create a knowledge platform to enable the proper implementation of the Act.

The Aaroh Campaign (*We Are the Women Farmers*) showed what mass mobilisation meant and what it could achieve. This project ran for nearly 10 years like a campaign for the rights of the women farmers in UP. It shattered patriarchal social norms and gave women farmers recognition and respect in society and the media.

India lagged behind on health and education parameters and these six states were the worst in the pack. And this was reason enough for Oxfam India to focus on these two essential services. Oxfam had already been a part of the Nine is Mine Campaign[2], so the next step was to work on the areas where this extra expenditure needed to go. Moreover, not many Oxfams globally worked on health and education, but India could because it had the freedom to work on these essential services.

For education, it moved beyond brick and mortar, and service delivery and ran individual projects in different states to ensure that no child was left behind (*Kuwar Gets Back To*

---

[2] The Nine is Mine Campaign was led by children across the country. This was one of the shining examples of Wada Na Todo Abhiyaan's (WNTA) mass mobilisation. The 'nine' refers to the 6 per cent of GDP on education plus the 3 per cent on health that children claimed as their right.

School). Through the health project (*Making Maternal Health Matter*), Oxfam India instead of looking at service delivery designed a multi-state project around the social determinants critical to maternal health. As an aside, this project built Oxfam India's capacity to write its own proposal and raise its own funds.

The networks and alliances (*Bringing Change, Together*) that it either formed or was a part of went on to prove that Oxfam India had been accepted and assimilated as part of the larger Indian civil society. When Oxfam India was formed (and other NGOs were setting up their Indian affiliate), there was also this concern among the civil society that NGOs like Oxfam who were donors would step on their shoes and jostle for fundraising space.

The last 10 years have shown that Oxfam India has done well to allay these fears. They continued backing organisations, forming networks and alliances and advocating for justice and dignity for all!

"*We cannot promise the moon but we should give them something to change their lives.*"

—Kiran Nanavati
OIN's Programme Coordinator,
Kosi Flood Recovery
2009–10

Kosi Flood Response and Recovery
Supaul, Bihar (2008–10)

The first time Oxfam came to India was in 1951 to respond to the Bihar famine. Call it a coincidence, but when Oxfam India (OIN) was born, it was in the midst of one of the worst floods in the history of India, also in Bihar. As the baton was being passed from Oxfam Great Britain (OGB) to OIN, it inherited the legacy of impeccable humanitarian response. And OIN was about to be tested!

Bihar is India's most flood-prone state with 76 per cent of its population in North Bihar plains living under the constant threat of recurring floods and the devastation in its aftermath. Bihar has faced severe floods since 1978 but the Kosi flood was the worst in the history of the country.

The state and aid agencies jumped into the response all guns blazing. Oxfam sourced in funds from its different affiliates, from the European Commission's Humanitarian Aid office and CSO partners as well as from the private sector like Microsoft India. Food, shelter, water and sanitation—everything was taken care of. Emphasis was laid on marginalised communities and women.

Although OGB conducted the initial assessment, both response and recovery became more personalised once OIN took over due to their ability to tune into local mores and cultural dynamics.

OIN reached out to nearly 38,000 families during the response and almost 6,700 families during the recovery phase. The ₹2.7 crore recovery project was planned for a 15-month period and the aim was to give social and economic stability and sustainability.

This was a significant response-recovery project on two counts. One, it turned out to be one of the worst floods affecting three million people in Bihar. The impact was worst in Supaul, in North Bihar, where the Kosi River breached its embankment in August and wreaked havoc. Two, it was also around the time when Oxfam India was born. The Kosi flood was a litmus test of OIN's capacity to take on a humanitarian project of this magnitude. And it excelled.

The story looks both at the speedy response in the first three months and the multifaceted recovery programme, which took place over nearly one and a half years. The recovery phase was particularly important to bring back social and economic stability, especially among the Dalits and Muslims, something which even 10 years later the community in Supaul gives Oxfam India credit for.

When Kosi Flooded Supaul

The Day of the Deluge

Dilip Kumar Jha sat in the portico of his house, on a cot, sifting through a sheaf of papers. Shambhu Nath Shaw and I were meeting Jha, the secretary of ward number 10 of Tekhuna Gram Panchayat. This was in Supaul district, nearly 250 km from Patna. Posters of gods and goddesses adorned the walls. The TV whirred from inside the house and the bulb hummed on the outside. Songs from a wedding, some distance away, flitted through the evening air. So did the incessant chirp of crickets.

Things were relatively quiet on this February evening, unlike almost 10 years ago.

Jha was one of the village volunteers in 2008 when Oxfam went in to respond to the Bihar floods. Kosi had breached its embankment at Kusaha in Nepal, changed its course and instead of flowing in the south-west direction flowed south, wreaking havoc in North Bihar's Supaul district. It reached Madhepura, Araria, Khagaria, Purnea and Saharsa as well. The Kosi has a heavy sediment load because of which it shifts course; it has shifted its course 160 km westward from the east of Purnea (in 1751) to east of Darbhanga (in 1950). There are 15 abandoned channels through which Kosi flowed, at different times, before the embankment was built.

The floods were unexpected. The barrage, which had the capacity to hold up to 0.9 million cusec of water, held 0.14 million cusec of water at the time of the breach. The breach was the result of sheer dereliction of duty on the part of the Indian engineers responsible for the upkeep of the Kosi barrage. This is well documented; signs of erosion had started showing up around 5 August but nothing was done about it.[1]

The floods, as per the official records, killed nearly 250 people, displaced three million and destroyed standing crops worth 0.3 million hectares.[2] The Kosi floods of 2008 proved to be the worst flood disaster in the history of independent India.[3]

Jha recalls hearing rumours of a breach on the evening of 17 August when he was at the Pratapganj market. Pratapganj and Simrahi Bazaar are the closest towns to Tekhuna Gram Panchayat. "I must have bought groceries worth ₹3,000 that day. I thought if the river does flood us, we should be prepared. Back home everyone said I was being an alarmist, that I had simply wasted money and that Kosi was not going to come to Supaul."

At around 6 AM on 18 August, he woke up to a commotion. Water was gushing past his house and with it were bundles of jute, trees, animals and dead bodies. Jha and his family had just enough time to move to the terrace, which was merely a tin

---

[1] Mishra, Dinesh Kumar, 'Bihar Floods: The Inevitable has Happened', *Economic & Political Weekly*, September 2008.

[2] Gupta, Alok, 'Kosi Flood Report Submitted, Finally', *Down to Earth*, March 2014, http://www.downtoearth.org.in/news/kosi-floods-inquiry-report-submitted-finally-43831 (as viewed on 13 April 2018).

[3] Chakrabarti, Rajesh, *Bihar Breakthrough: The Turnaround of a Beleaguered State*, March 2013, pp. 178–79.

shed back then. But it was big enough to accommodate four of them and nine of his other relatives. The water in and around his house nearly rose to 7 feet. "There was mayhem all around." He was still among the lucky ones. In other places, the water was almost 15 feet high.

Oxfam India's First Challenge

Back in Delhi, there were churnings of another sort. Oxfam was going through its own transition of becoming an independent affiliate in India. OGB, which was working in India at that time as the largest affiliate, was in the process of handing over and giving shape to what would be called Oxfam India. As some old-timers put it, the question wasn't whether it had to respond, the question was how it would respond.

Nisha Agrawal became the CEO on 1 March 2008. For the next six months, she worked closely with a consulting agency to get a smooth handover from all the six affiliates for OIN. OIN was formed on 1 September 2008. Kosi breached the embankment on 18 August 2008.

The humanitarian response had always been, and continues to be, the crowning glory for Oxfam.

When the transition happened, humanitarian remained a sticky issue with OGB. They were reluctant to give away humanitarian to OIN. "They wanted to lead the Kosi response because they weren't confident that OIN, a new organisation, could handle it. This despite the fact that the staff would technically remain the same," says Nisha.

Nisha recalls how they kept saying, "OIN wouldn't know what to do. You will perhaps kill people." OIN offered to take OGB's help in case of CAT II disaster—Kosi was CAT II—but insisted that they would lead the response.

Supaul was the worst affected and therefore the obvious choice for a response from Oxfam. The effect was worse because the very embankment that was supposed to protect them had breached. Supaul, Saharsa and Madhepura had not expected such a breach and were therefore not well equipped to fight floods the way Araria and Begusarai were (Oxfam Novib and Oxfam Hong Kong responded in the other districts).

The Bihar government brought in their go-to flood man, N Saravana Kumar, on 20 August. He was initially posted as the additional district magistrate (DM) of Supaul to aid the response work but was soon given the sole charge of the district.[4] He had very efficiently dealt with Samastipur floods as the DM just a year ago.

Relief Camps and Rescue Ops

Nearly 2.5 million people and 441 villages of the six districts were the worst affected; more than a million people were displaced within the first five days.[5] People had taken shelter on high grounds and embankments.

---

[4] Chakrabarti, Rajesh, *Bihar Breakthrough: The Turnaround of a Beleaguered State*, March 2013, pp. 178–79.

[5] Oxfam India's 'Bihar Floods 2008 – Rapid Assessment Report', filed on 25 August 2008.

OIN along with its partners, Bihar Seva Samiti (BSS) and Abhigyan Disha[6] assessed four relief camps in Basantpur block (Bhim Nagar Chowk, Lalpur village, Katayia powerhouse and 22 RD camp) and one in Pratapganj block (Belhi camp). A back of the envelope calculation showed that nearly 20,000 families were at these camps along roadsides and embankments. As rescue operations were picking up, both by government and the NGOs, more were expected to turn up. Supaul district administration ran 77 relief camps.[7]

Oxfam completed its assessment by 23 August. The nod was given that very day and Oxfam started its relief work. Between 24 August and 26 August, stocks were brought in from the warehouse at Madhubani; later they were brought in from other places as well. The state government called its first Inter-Agency Group (IAG) meeting on 27 August. This was a meeting of all government organisations and NGOs to assess and appraise the situation and identify the area that each organisation would take up to avoid duplication of relief operations. In fact, these meetings became a weekly affair. Kumar's posting was a blessing for NGOs; passes to aid workers and approvals to distribute relief material were promptly issued.

The state brought in the army and air force for the rescue operations, but the lack of rescue boats was hindering evacuation

---

[6] Due to financial irregularities on their part, Oxfam left both the partners within a month and did direct implementation.

[7] Chakrabarti, Rajesh, *Bihar Breakthrough: The Turnaround of a Beleaguered State*, March 2013, pp. 178–79.

operations of stranded men, women and children from villages to relief camps. The state government approached Oxfam and its partners to provide rescue boats. Oxfam dispatched two motorised boats to Araria and one to Supaul. Oxfam had used rescue boats in the 2007 floods and they were parked at its warehouse in Madhubani.[8]

By 31 August, Oxfam started its relief operation.

When Radha Cinema Became a Warehouse

The flood was devastating and the casualties high; a high-speed response was planned. All hands were brought on board. While stocks of non-food items like tarpaulin and groundsheets were at the Madhubani warehouse, food had to be procured. Funds were needed. An appeal for funds was issued by Oxfam India.

The stocks from Madhubani warehouse were brought into Supaul through a circuitous route (from the north-west) since most access routes were flooded. As supplies came in, they were being stored in a house that was turned into a temporary warehouse.

While funds were awaited, Shambhu Nath recalls an initial amount of ₹5 lakh being sanctioned by the then Oxfam's Eastern India regional manager, the late Lal Chand Garg to start procurement of food immediately; it was purchased from neighbouring districts as well as from Kolkata. In the

---

[8] 'Oxfam India issues appeal: Scales up response to Bihar floods', *Citizen News Service*, 1 September 2008, http://www.citizen-news.org/2008/09/oxfam-india-issues-appeal-scales-up.html (as viewed on 16 April 2018).

meantime, a more permanent and accessible warehouse was being scouted for at Simrahi Bazaar.

Simrahi Bazaar, a town in the Raghopur block, stands at the intersection of the National Highway 131 and the East-West corridor that runs from Porbandar to Silchar. This was the dry zone and it used to be chock-a-block every day with people clutching onto their valuables and heading to the relief camps. Camps were set up on either side of the highway.

Not very far from the bustling main market at Simrahi Bazaar, Shambhu Nath takes us to Radha Cinema Hall. The only telltale signs are a ticket counter and a now-showing film poster. The building, with living quarters on the first floor, has a tall black grill and a fresh coat of white paint on the outside.

"This became our warehouse. This was on dry land, was on the main road and was accessible. Perfect to keep the stocks that were being brought in from all over the country. The hall inside was vacant, barring three rows of benches fixed at the back, which were the 'VIP seats'. The rest of the hall had plastic chairs that could be removed. We negotiated with the hall owner and offered him to pay half of what he would have earned monthly if he ran houseful every day. He agreed. Every penny counted," says Shambhu Nath. Back then, Shambhu Nath was the logistics assistant with the humanitarian team.

The hall was still the same even after 10 years—a double-panelled door, dark and dirty curtains, and beyond the curtains, the same darkness. A few seconds later, as the eyes adjust to the darkness, the three rows of fixed benches become visible. The plastic chairs are lined up on the side.

The cinema hall had served its purpose back then. Once the response started on 25 August, the first lot of non-food items—tarpaulin, groundsheets, blankets, water purifying solutions like zeoline and halogen tablets, buckets, chlorination units, tube wells, latrine units—were brought in from Madhubani and stocked in Radha Cinema Hall.

"The availability of contingency stocks meant that we were one of the first to respond without losing any time," says Zubin Zaman, the humanitarian manager back then. Diagonally opposite the cinema hall was Lakshmi Guest House—a hotel/lodge—that had become the base camp for the next three months for Oxfam India and the other humanitarian agencies.

Food, Water and Shelter

Tarpaulin and groundsheets were distributed in 22 RD, Bhim Nagar Chowk, Belhi and Katayia relief camps. "We had just given the tent material. Those in the camps immediately set up bamboo poles and made their tents. We didn't even have to tell them," says Shambhu Nath.

Vijay Kumar 'Babloo' recalls seeing tents with Oxfam logos all around. Vijay was volunteering around the same time through another organisation. He later joined Purvanchal Gramin Vikas Sansthan (PGVS), one of the NGO partners of Oxfam that rolled out the Kosi recovery programme later in 2009.

Blankets were brought in for distribution keeping in mind the approaching winters. But Oxfam (as did the other organisations) did not get permission to distribute them at the camps. And this was perhaps because the government wasn't expecting the camps to continue into the winters. People started moving back to their villages in the second half of October. These blankets were then distributed among the marginalised communities, who were also the worst affected, in the villages in Sukhanagar, Suryapur, Tekhuna and Bhawanipur panchayats. This was done between September and mid-December.

Food distribution began as soon as the warehouse was in place. A few days into the relief camps, the only food that the displaced were getting was a one-time meal of *khichdi* provided by the locals. With pregnant women, lactating mothers and children in the camp, it became imperative to distribute ready-to-eat dry food to wade off the imminent danger of hunger and starvation facing everyone right in their faces.

Food packets comprising *chiwda* (beaten rice), *sattu* (gram flour), *gur* (jaggery), groundnut, salt and biscuits (two packets) were distributed. This was the staple local diet but more importantly, it did not need to be cooked. And in the scenario, where people were living on rooftops and in camps, this was the most feasible option. These packets had candles and matchboxes as well. These were distributed at relief camps. Those like Jha who had refused to leave their homes came to the camps to collect their food packets.

So did Mohammed Isaar Ahmed from the neighbouring Suryapur Panchayat. Ahmed and most in his village refused to leave. Like Jha's family, they too were confident that the floods would bypass Suryapur. "Thc floods reached our village by noon. Most of the village was under 4 feet of water, some low lying areas were submerged up to 10 feet. People huddled on cots and terraces. It was the holy month of Ramzan but far from celebrations, it had become a matter of survival," says Ahmed, who we met in his village in 2018.

Apart from the relief camps, Oxfam and its partners were distributing food simultaneously to three panchayats—Sukhanagar, Suryapur and Bhawanipur. Though they did distribute food packets to Suryapur Panchayat, they weren't able to reach Ahmed's village. His village was completely cut-off and surrounded by floodwater. Boats were few and people used drums and trunk of banana plants as boats to reach to drier areas in Simrahi and the camps for food and medicines. This was also their mode of transport for ferrying out relatives who were visiting for Ramzan but were caught in the floods.

As the water began to recede, community kitchens began to spring up; the government, political parties and NGOs set up a total of 21 community kitchens. Two meals of boiled rice, *dal* and vegetable curry per day were provided at these community kitchens.[9] According to government data, nearly 1,00,000 people were fed daily for 45 days.[10] The food packets supplemented the freshly cooked food; Oxfam distributed food from 9 September.

With food and shelter taken care of, providing safe drinking water was on high priority. This was critical to avoid the spread

---

[9] Oxfam India's 'Bihar Floods 2008 – Rapid Assessment Report', filed on 25 August 2008.

[10] Chakrabarti, Rajesh, *Bihar Breakthrough: The Turnaround of a Beleaguered State*, March 2013, pp. 178–79.

of water-borne diseases. In the camps, hand pumps were few and shallow. In the villages, the hand pumps were submerged, leaving families with no access to safe drinking water. Jha recalls that during the initial days, people were drinking floodwater and using it to soak rice overnight to be able to eat it the next day—the same floodwater in which people were forced to defecate.

"Cases of diarrhoea and cholera had started to come up in camps and villages. But it was quickly contained. ORS solutions and zeoline tablets were distributed. Filtered water was provided in the camps. So we used to go to the camps to collect water," recalls Jha. The government, too, did its bit—halogen tablets were airdropped along with food packets.

Within a few days, Oxfam installed a water filtration machine. This potable water was then taken to Belhi camps via tractors. Apart from the water filter, nearly 287 tube wells were dug during the three months of the response. Almost 109 tube wells were dug at the four camps and the remaining in Tekhuna, Suryapur and Sukhanagar panchayats once people started moving back to the villages. Apart from setting up tube wells, Oxfam ensured that existing tube wells were repaired and disinfected and those damaged, during floods, were decommissioned.

Reaching out to nearly 38,000 families couldn't have been made possible without volunteers. They were identified from within the displaced families and were paid a daily stipend; in the initial days, they worked for nearly eight hours every day, which was reduced to five hours for six days every week. The volunteers were trained to create awareness on good hygiene practices, water chlorination, hand washing, proper disposal of waste as well as disease surveillance.

This work continued into the recovery phase, which started in 2009. The success of the continuous work around WASH (Water and Sanitation Hygiene) can be gauged from what a villager said in a documentary *Koshi Katha*. "Earlier no one washed their hands before eating—neither children nor adults. But now they wash their hands with soap. Now that is a change."

Ahmed and Jha were two of the many volunteers. During the response, when the water levels started receding in the villages, the fear of a breakout of diseases once again reared its ugly head. "There was muck everywhere. It stank. We went to the nearby hospitals, got bleaching powder and used it to decontaminate our streets, homes, tube wells. Drinking water was still scarce. We remember going about with zeoline solutions and halogen tablets to ensure that no one is left out," says Ahmed.

In order to stop the contamination of water, it was important to stop open defecation. Sanitation and hygiene were totally compromised; toilets and bathing spaces needed to be created. Women, especially, were the worst affected. They not only had to go to relieve themselves in the dark, but also had to scout for safe places in the congested campsites. Consultations were held with women and girls; latrines and bathing cubicles were constructed keeping their need for privacy and safety in mind.

In fact, the women came up with a similar demand for their panchayats. Oxfam continued this in the recovery phase as well when community bathrooms were constructed in the three panchayats. Committees were formed for their upkeep. During one of the meetings, it came to light that because minor repairs of hand pumps took a long time, women faced difficulty without water. So it was decided to train women to repair minor glitches in the hand pumps. Around 24 women hand-pump mechanics were trained; 13 belonged to the Dalit and Adivasi community.

Over 1,100 latrines, 250 of which were in the camps, and 440 bathing cubicles were constructed. "Once the camps were evacuated, these temporary latrines and bathing cubicles were demolished, decomposed and covered with sand. This is an emergency protocol," explains Shambhu Nath. In the panchayats, Oxfam selected houses of marginalised communities—Dalits and Muslims. Demo units were built using mud and bamboo; these were economical and simple to build.

During the last visit in 2018, these latrines had long been dismantled. But the units built at that time created awareness and encouraged people to build permanent, private latrines and bathing spaces. "Most houses have either built toilets on their own or through government schemes," says Ahmed.

The River of Sorrow Brought Sand, Not Silt

Most of the families displaced in these camps were from the marginalised communities. The wealthier families either moved to other villages or rented a house in the town or those like Jha stayed put in their own homes because they had proper homes with proper roofs.

People lost homes and livelihoods. In most cases, floods bring silt and are good for crops. But the Kosi brought sand with it. Not only were the standing crops completely decimated and buried under five feet of water at some places, once the water receded, the accumulated sand left the once fertile fields uncultivable.

In this scenario, the creation of immediate employment opportunity was imperative. Once the water level receded, Oxfam engaged locals to construct tube wells and latrines. This helped bring back some hope in the lives of those who had lost their sources of livelihood to the floods. Jha remembers one of the organisations carrying out a 'food for work' programme where food was given in exchange for dredging sand out of the fields.

In most cases, people are still coping with the loss of land even after 10 years. Layers of grey-silver sand could still be seen as we drove through the 2008 flood-affected villages in February 2018. Those who could dredge it out, did it; others were either too poor or incapable to get it done. To explain the extent of the 'sand' problem, Vijay draws a parallel between Rajasthan's Thar Desert and Balua Bazaar in Birpur (one of the worst affected towns of Supaul district on the Bihar-Nepal border).

Usually, the rains that follow are expected to wash the sand away. But, in this case, it had to be removed manually or mechanically. Paromita Chowdhury, Eastern India's regional manager, who led the recovery phase of the Kosi flood response programme in 2009, said in a recent interview, "Oxfam didn't work on land rejuvenation. And perhaps this needed aggressive rehabilitation."

Oxfam may not have worked on land reclamation but it did everything else possible to ensure that villagers were rehabilitated. And they ticked all the correct boxes. For the recovery phase, Oxfam India bought on board two organisations—PGVS and Nidan.

Planning the Recovery

The response was formally closed in December 2008 and this was marked by a series of meetings with Supaul administration, cross-border learning between India and Nepal (OGB, through its staff in Kathmandu, had responded to the Nepal side of the floods) and handing over of infrastructure to the panchayat and local government.

During the four months in 2008, Oxfam India had gradually eased into OGB's big humanitarian shoes. It conducted a recovery assessment, similar to relief assessment done at the beginning of the response. People had lost their land, homes, loved ones and livelihoods to the flood. A disease outbreak was lurking around the corner. If the community had to bounce back, people had to be supported in multiple ways.

And it had to be done quickly enough to ensure that the community, especially the marginalised, does not fall in the trap of moneylenders. Thus, for the OIN, time was of the essence.

It was decided that OIN would go back to three panchayats—Suryapur, Sukhanagar and Tekhuna—in 2009, to work on livelihoods, public health and disaster risk reduction.

A recovery phase was required to not just bring back economic stability but also social stability. It was also important that any work that Oxfam India did with the community built their resilience and had a long-term impact. "Fifteen months wasn't going to change everything, but we surely worked towards making some difference in their lives. Something that would continue even after we exited," says Kiran Nanavati, a consultant earlier with OGB who was roped in by OIN as programme coordinator for the Kosi flood recovery project.

The project started in February 2009. But with elections scheduled in April, the district administration had ordered a clamp down on all work citing code of conduct. There was no time for a hit and trial, so these months were used to assess, draw a blueprint and plan down to the last detail.

The better off managed to reclaim their land enough to bounce back to some extent (though they needed some agricultural support as well). It was the people from the marginalised communities, the daily wage labourers and artisans who suffered a major setback; the artisans either lost their tools or they were damaged. Then there were the single, widowed women who had lost their husbands to the flood or earlier and had nothing left to support their families.

This presented an opportunity for a livelihood project including agriculture-based rehabilitation work. A part of the livelihood project was about getting villagers back on their feet by distributing livelihood toolkits; the agriculture-based rehabilitation project, as the name suggests, wanted to rehabilitate the setback received in agriculture and allied activities. This would later evolve into livestock distribution and seed fair.

That these were not planned at the outset of the recovery project is, in fact, one of the positive outcomes of the shift from OGB to OIN. While OGB came with a lot of experience and professional expertise, with OIN, the recovery became more organic, flexible and in sync with the local needs. Whether it was the issue of caste or gender or livelihoods—local conditions were taken into consideration and a best-case scenario was proposed.

"The humanitarian team had no prior experience of an agriculture-based rehabilitation project. But one of our funders, CSO Partners[11], was quite keen and deeply involved in strengthening the project. This was a very good opportunity to rebuild agriculture. Moreover, Nand Kishore Singh and Kiran proved very resourceful with their experience," says Paromita. Nand Kishore was a part of the livelihood team, specialising in agriculture; Kiran had experience of semi-arid farming.

The agriculture-based rehabilitation project was parked for later and it would need some strategic planning. The livelihood project, on the other hand, seemed pretty straightforward.

[11] ICICI funded Oxfam's recovery project through CSO Partners.

Oxfam would have to simply identify the artisans and their needs and distribute the toolkits.

But it wasn't as straightforward as it seemed.

Walking a Tightrope

A village committee was proposed to increase community involvement and with their help understand the ward structure, livelihood patterns and livestock holdings. A survey was planned to identify villagers who were worst affected and needed support. Like during the response, for recovery too, village volunteers would be selected to conduct the survey.

But all this was easier said than done. The vulnerability of the marginalised communities, lack of employment opportunities, the rigid caste and power dynamics, deep gender biases and the possibility of the influential castes appropriating the entire distribution process posed very serious concerns. Moreover, the Lok Sabha elections due in April–May 2009 further emboldened the power dynamics and deepened the caste divide.

"Villages had been swept away, people had lost everything they had and they were divided along caste lines. So it was extremely important to build strong foundations and mend this fracture. The rich guys could get hurt. So it was important to work our way around these sensitive systems without getting hurt in the process," explains Paromita.

The team knew that this would be akin to walking on eggshells. So systems were put in place. Having worked closely with the three panchayats during the response months, OIN along with the two partners built on the rapport and held extensive community meetings.

"We did not just want to give the hardware part of it, that is, service delivery, we also wanted to give them the software part of it, that is, raise awareness. This was long term. We wanted to build the resilience of the community," says Kiran. In other words, the Village Disaster Preparedness Committees (VDPCs) were formed to promote leadership, equity and transparency.

These meetings were meant to communicate to the community the idea of recovery, mobilise them and form the VDPC. These meetings and committees were looked upon as a medium to bridge the class, caste and gender gap.

The Banyan Tree

When the committees were being formed, the process laid bare the initial concerns and apprehensions. Participation from the marginalised communities and women was found wanting. Extra effort was made to make them the core of the VDPC. Meetings were held with women, men, marginalised communities, upper caste and village panchayats to drive home the point that villages would be rebuilt in an equitable and equal manner.

Village volunteers conducted the livelihood survey. These villages mostly had masons, potters, carpenters, basket and mat weavers, tailors, painters, petty shop owners and vendors and those who repaired cycles. Artisans were selected on the basis of criteria laid out for toolkit distribution—they had to be flood-affected, should have lost their toolkit and belonged to the Dalit and Mahadalit community. Single, widowed women who had lost their source of income were also included in the list. In fact, similar criteria were drawn for the livestock distribution; the added benchmark was that they had cattle and had lost it, or had knowledge about rearing cattle; preference was given to single women.

First, lists were drawn by volunteers and village committees. OIN staff later vetted them. "Initially, when the lists started coming in, we realised that it was influenced by the dominant castes and the marginalised were actually being left out," says Vijay.

Some more meetings were held. Some more mobilisation and tact were needed. Then came the idea of the banyan tree!

The villagers along with the committee members were called for mettings under banyan or peepal trees. People revere these trees; they believe that if they lie under the banyan tree, some ill fate will befall them. "There, under the tree, we would go through the list with them and ask them to judge for themselves if there was anyone who should not be on the list. People actually started coming up and saying that they don't need to be on the list. This trick worked."

Once the process of identifying 'project participants' was ironed out—Kiran in a recent phone conversation emphasised that this was done to avoid terms such as beneficiaries—Oxfam India did its own due diligence. Home visits were made to confirm the veracity of the list. Muster rolls were prepared and project participant cards distributed. Both had photos; this was to ensure that the toolkits went to the right people. And it did. There were very strict protocols about giving kits and livestock to only those whose photo was on the muster roll. Exceptions were made for the differently-abled.

Saws, Spades and Sickles

As we went about meeting people—Shambhu Nath, Vijay, Jha and I—we heard murmurs of "इसे तो हम पहचानते हैं" ("*We know this*"). They were pointing at the green Oxfam logo on my black bag. A few pleasantries were exchanged. Many recognised Shambhu Nath and Vijay. "बड़ी कंपनी आयी थी और सामान भी दिया था" ("*Big company was here and they gave us things*"), says Najam Bhai who met us at ward number 13 of Sukhanagar Panchayat. The सामान were the livelihood toolkits. The बड़ी कंपनी was Oxfam India. Najam got a labourers toolkit.

"At that time, getting the tools would have cost us a substantial amount—up to ₹1,500. And in some cases, we wouldn't even have got it easily. Spending that kind of money at that time would have been unthinkable for most of us. This was extremely important to get us back on our feet," says Ahmed, joined in by the others at Suryapur. The toolkits were distributed in steel trunks; which provided for extra sturdy storage. A few families we visited in 2018, still had the steel trunk and the toolkits.

"We could get back to work immediately. Soon after the floods receded, houses had to be repaired, furniture had to be made. There was a lot of scope for work and had we not got the tools then, we would have taken much longer to get back on our feet," says Bhuwaneshwar Sharma, of Badhai tola, ward number 11, Tekhuna. Other carpenters and masons who had gathered at his house concurred.

Sharma, seated on a chair, probably one of those he made himself, asked one of his grandchildren to get the trunk from inside the house. The trunk, with the sticker of Oxfam India-PGVS-CSO Partners still intact, had the carpentry tools. Sharma still uses it and so do his sons.

Not very far from Sharma's house is Zulekha Khatoon's grocery shop. She was given a kit to start a tea stall and a grocery store. Zulekha and her husband were farm labourers and in the aftermath of the floods, there wasn't much work left in the fields. Her Indira Aawas Yojana home was mostly swept away in the floods; but she and her family of eight had refused to leave her house or whatever was left of it, to go to the camps. They survived it, having lived on a cot and later a *machaan* for those few months.

The tea stall continued for a few months but her grocery store has flourished. "I had to stop the tea stall. People would drink and not give money," she smiles. But her grocery store is still thriving. Her husband and sons work as migrant labourers. Zulekha adds, "People may not always have money, so we have an understanding that they would sometimes give me grain or vegetables. It works fine."

Nearly 40 per cent of the toolkits—especially mat-making and basket-weaving kits—were almost entirely given to women. This was a first for some; it gave them economic independence and the confidence to support their families and reduce their vulnerabilities.

Apart from the toolkits, those who had some patch of homestead land were given a set of tools and a bag of vegetable seeds to start a kitchen garden. Nutrition is, after all, an essential cog in public health wheel. The tools included a spade, sickle and a basket. The idea was to ensure that they could grow some basic vegetables, organically as much as possible, get the much-needed nourishment and if there were extra it would serve as additional income.

These were just a handful of seeds. OIN was planning something bigger.

Jha—Tekhuna's Radish Man

As we settled at Jha's house the next day for lunch, he insisted we especially taste the *mooli* in the salad. The *mooli* was from his field; the seeds for which he first got at the seed fair organised by OIN. He grows it on the furrows in his wheat field. He also grows Simran wheat; again from the seed fair.

"Simran in the first year gave less than 8 quintals per acre, but soon it started giving up to 12 quintals. We were farming earlier also but after Kosi completely ravaged our field, the seed fair invited Krishi Vigyan Kendra (KVK) officials who advised us on what to grow and how. That was very useful," says Jha, who latched on to the concept of intercropping after OIN organised the seed fair. He has now become the go-to man for radish in the village.

Agriculture had received a major setback due to the floods—crops had been destroyed and the land rendered uncultivable. Farming in the region was limping back—those who could reclaim their land did so, others were trying to sustain themselves by farming on small patches of homestead land. While Oxfam didn't work on land reclamation, it wanted to ensure that farmers at least had access to the basic raw material—seeds.

Consultations were held with individual experts as well as with NGOs such as Udaipur-based Jagran Jan Vikas Samiti (JJVS) that had held seed fairs in the past. They trained the partners. A seed fair was preferred to seed distribution. "A farmer knows what is best for his field, what he can grow and what he wants in any given scenario. It was crucial that they choose what they want and buy according to their needs," says Nand Kishore.

Seed companies were brought to the fair; three seed fairs were organised in the three panchayats. Villagers were informed of the dates in advance. A central location was chosen for easy access to everyone in the panchayat. In Tekhuna, the seed fair was held in a school quite close to Jha's house. Nearly 1,500 coupons were distributed.

According to the documentary *Koshi Katha,* 50 per cent of the coupons were given to marginalised communities and nearly 30 per cent to Dalits and Adivasis. The farmers could choose from a range of seeds—from potatoes and onions to maize and all kinds of vegetables. The turnout was huge.

Despite the fact that a few seemed to miss their favourite Anil seeds—"Anil बीजा होता तो वही लेते। ये भी ठीक है।"—the fair was a massive success.

The seed fair achieved a few things—one, it provided farmers with access to seeds and seed companies; two, it brought in agricultural scientists from nearby KVK for trainings; three, it provided exposure to women and children who could learn about seeds and take independent decisions especially when their husbands migrated; and, four, it promoted organic, low-cost agriculture.

The bar had been set high. And this was going to be bettered in April and May, the following year.

Rasheedan's Goat

Villagers had lost their livestock in the floods; for some their main source of income. Most in these villages had cattle. "Villagers were cash-strapped. When we did a needs assessment, those who didn't have the experience of keeping cattle, were eager to keep small livestock such as goats," says Paromita.

Oxfam India decided to hold livestock distribution—cow-calf pairs as well as goats. Paromita mentions in our recent phone conversation that this was uncharted territory and not planned at the outset of the recovery project. This was in 2010, at the fag end of the recovery project.

So Nand Kishore and Kiran stepped in. Shambhu Nath played a key role in the procurement of the livestock; in 2008, he was the logistics assistant with the Eastern India office in Kolkata. In retrospect, Shambhu Nath says, the livestock procurement and distribution being carried out for the first time by OIN could have turned into a logistical disaster.

Though it kept the team on their toes, it was worth it.

Consultations were held with organisations with experience in livestock distribution. The breed of the cow and calf and its quality were key. It was decided that the livestock should be a local breed, should be a second-calf cow, the calf should be no more than a month old and the cow should be able to give five litres of milk daily. Shambhu Nath explains that first-calf cows give very little milk and the quantity substantially reduces after the third calf. The milch cow is at its best in its second-calf stage.

A procurement tender (for the fodder as well) was floated. Shambhu Nath remembers that the initial plan was to distribute it to 1,000 families; this was reduced to 336 families due to budget constraints. But, the quality wasn't compromised. The village committees were involved in the entire process—from choosing the best local variety to overseeing the tender process, from procurement to distribution—making it a very transparent exercise. The livestock was distributed to project participants from 23 villages in two panchayats as per the criteria laid out.

The vetting of this list too was done under the banyan tree!

An agriculture field, close to the Lakshmi Guest House at Simrahi Bazaar, was taken on rent to serve as the cowshed. The cows and their calves were brought to the cowshed in lots of about 60 and kept for 5–6 days. "The journey is traumatic for cows and they are bound to produce less or no milk. They need to relax and be calm for a few days," says Shambhu Nath.

"A couple of days after the first lot of cows arrived, they were milked in the morning for monitoring. That gave us about 150 litres of milk (about 300 litres a day), which we distributed among all passers-by. Next morning, a crowd was waiting, each holding a vessel for collecting milk!" Nanavati says. That day, a decision was taken to provide milk to all students in the nearby school.

Oxfam had a built-in return policy on the condition that the cow did not give the stipulated amount of milk during the time it was kept at the cowshed. During such time that the cow was rested for distribution; project participants were selected for that round. The most marginalised were selected first. In order to make the distribution fair and transparent, the cows were tagged and these numbers were put out for draw of lots. The project participants as per the muster roll would come to the cowshed and pick a number. That lucky draw decided their livestock. Some went home happy, some not so pleased (especially if they got a male calf), but no one could complain that it wasn't a fair process.

Back then, to be doubly sure that there were no oversights, the team conducted surprise night visits at homes with lists. "This was to make sure that the livestock has actually gone to the family mentioned on the list," says Shambhu Nath. He and Kiran were part of the team that would set out on these surprise checks.

The cow-calf pairs were distributed along with the fodder; the fodder was for three months. Within three months, families were able to reap benefits and buy feed by themselves. Para-vet camps were held; a few from the community were trained to be para-vets. The cows and calves were insured. A few availed the insurance when the cows died.

As we were walking through the village, a few recognised Shambhu Nath and Vijay and came up to them to complain. The villagers said they hadn't got their insurance money when their cow died. Notwithstanding the number of years that had gone by—eight years—both of them gave a very patient ear. Probing a little further, it came to light that most did not follow the steps that were required to get the insurance money, that is, getting a certificate from a vet immediately, for starters. These were just a handful of cases. Many had followed the steps and received the money.

During our 2018 visit, the calves and its offspring were very much there. Most of the people we spoke to, told us how it took care of their domestic nutritional needs and income. A few we met had sold off the offspring to fund marriages, medical treatments and education.

Overall, the villagers were happy with the *maveshi* that the *badi* company gave. But things were a little different on the goat front. Over a 1,000 goats were distributed—she-goats weighing at least 8–9 kg and in good health. We bumped into one Rasheedan Khatoon in Tekhuna who still had the goat with her. Rasheedan has lost count of the number of kids the goat gave birth to; one of her nieces recalls selling almost 13 kids over the years.

"We sold them. They fetched us a good price and that took care of our children's education." Rasheedan stays in a large joint family and all of them together got three she-goats, of which only one survived. Most of the goats didn't survive; in fact, many say that Rasheedan's was the only one that survived. It could have been because of the cold. Some believed that because it was from a different district, it failed to adjust in these parts. Jha says that perhaps the goats were fed *sattu* and that did not suit them.

Paromita, however, thinks otherwise. Oxfam had taken extra precaution and provided veterinarian services for the cattle and goats. "And we had factored in all kinds of wastage probabilities. The goats were perhaps eaten within a few weeks! The cow was taken extra care of because they earned quite a bit from milk production."

Whatever the fate of the goats and the cows, the community cannot but vouch for the fair and flawless distribution, and the relevance of the distribution at that time.

And that stands true even after so many years.

Maybe Not the Moon

Though humanitarian response and recovery changed hands from OGB to OIN, the core essence of the programme—'we cannot promise the moon but we should give them something to change their lives'—remained.

For all of Oxfam's response and recovery, apart from shelter and food, WASH was and remains standard protocol. In Kosi's response and recovery too, Oxfam invested a substantial amount of time and human resources not just in giving away the services but also training the community and volunteers, especially the youth, on elements of WASH to integrate it into the very fabric of the community that was reeling under a disaster and limping back to normalcy.

What OIN also did was to dexterously tackle the very local and pertinent issues of caste, religion and gender. A case in point is the allocation of work for the volunteers. Their reluctance to work with each other or for each other stemmed from deep-set social norms.

"There was a mix of Brahmins, Yadavs, Dalits and Muslim volunteers. They were moved around quite a bit. For instance, the Brahmin volunteers were given the responsibility of Dalit areas; the Yadav volunteer was assigned the Muslim village and so on and so forth. There were inhibitions initially but once the work started, the focus and priority for everyone was providing the best for the community," says Vijay. For him, it was the first recovery project and also his first lesson on working around these social constructs.

The recovery phase was also a chance to train the lens of social equity and equality on the community and plan accordingly. A luxury that high-speed response could not have. "There were instances where upper caste influential people in the village amassed a lot of benefits during the flood response. But that is just in the nature of response," explains Paromita.

In one of the villages, a hand pump was fixed in the house of the upper caste landlord, which was located at the very start of the village. This was not accessible to the Dalit families. "When the team went for recovery assessment they drew a lot of flak. So assurances were given and extra care was taken to set things right in the recovery phase," explains Paromita.

Thus, the meetings with villagers, forming committees with the marginalised and women at its core and working on providing social and economic stability became the guiding points for OIN. Moreover, the Indianness made the recovery much more organic.

"The team was young and energetic. Due credit goes to OIN which was very flexible and so there was a chance to experiment with a lot of ideas. In fact, Kosi flood response and recovery project set a lot of precedents," says Paromita towards the end of our conversation.

Pandora's Box

The 2008 Kosi floods opened the veritable Pandora's Box for Supaul. But just as the last thing left in the box was 'hope' in a very ironical way, the floods too brought some hope. The floods brought the district into the sharp focus of the civil society.

Prior to 2008, Oxfam had not worked in the district; in fact, there was hardly any NGO or INGO presence. "This was an unknown area of work. When response and recovery started, the vulnerabilities of Supaul and specifically of the three panchayats stood exposed. With the work that followed, a lot of the villagers look at Kosi floods as a blessing," says Paromita.

For women, it spelt new employment opportunities—with basket-weaving and mat-making kits, this was the first time that they had a source of income. And the hope of a better future. For communities, there was infrastructure like toilets and tube wells and the knowhow of disaster preparedness. Issues of caste, religion and gender are deep-set and come with rigid biases. They are difficult to shake off. But the response and recovery showed that if guided well, communities could be brought together to work for a common cause.

That people still remember the logo, the *badi* company and the people involved is a testimony to the relevance of the work that was carried out.

लोग टूट जाते हैं एक घर बनाने में
तुम तरस नहीं खाते बस्तियां जलाने में।

—**बशीर बद्र**

"People work all through their lives to make their own homes;
And you don't even flinch for a moment before burning down
the whole village (township/borough/settlement)."

Conflict Response
Bodoland Territorial Area District (BTAD)–2012 and
Muzaffarnagar–2013

Any conflict—ethnic, communal or religious—rips apart the very fabric of society. There are perpetrators and then there are the affected. There are no winners. From a humanitarian perspective, conflicts are tricky to respond to. How will the organisation be perceived? What does one respond with? How far does one go? And who will fund conflict relief and response?

Oxfam India responded to two conflicts, both very different in kind. The first one was the Assam conflict in BTAD in 2012. The actual genesis of the July incident is unclear, but the larger issue is that of conflict over resources. And this was one in a series of a long history of violence wherein the indigenous Bodos have, for decades, felt cornered by the Muslims and the Santhals. The growing population has made matters worse and escalated tensions between the communities.

The Muzaffarnagar riots broke out in 2013. Uttar Pradesh has always been India's communal tinderbox. An eve-teasing incident turned into murder and then flared into one of the worst communal riots in the country. The majority Hindu killed, burnt, raped and looted the minority Muslims. It was purely communal and it had been simmering, with incidents of sporadic violence against Muslims, for over a year.

In both cases, families were forced to flee their homes and live in refugee camps. The difference was that in Assam, they came back to their villages, while in Muzaffarnagar, they made the refugee camps their home.

Very few aid agencies had any presence as most preferred to stay away from responding to conflict. While it wasn't easy to work under the constant glare of religious and political leaders, Oxfam India managed to deliver the best assistance possible to the most vulnerable and marginalised. Oxfam India carried out the response and the recovery work in both places without discriminating against any religious or ethnic groups. This, in the long run, particularly in Bodoland, brought communities together. Seeing an aid agency work without any biases became a catalyst for the communities to come back and live together.

Oxfam India proved its mettle in the area of conflict response.

A Tale of Two Conflicts

Whose Land Is It Anyway?

In February 2018, we visited Kokrajhar in Assam. I was visiting the survivors of an ethnic violence outbreak that erupted in 2012. Though the outbreak, on the face of it, looked communal—Muslims versus Bodos—it was actually a resource conflict. Oxfam India was there in the relief camps and later in the villages, 2012 onwards; this was the first time they responded to a conflict.

Vinuthna Patibandla (in charge of the Assam projects) and I headed to Shimultapu village in Kokrajhar. A few kilometres away, across the Sankosh River, is the West Bengal border. The village has a mix of Bodos and Muslims and was one of those villages where houses were burnt and looted in July 2012. But thankfully there were no deaths.

We were visiting Jhorna Narzary and some of her neighbours.

"We left on a Saturday night. The night of 21 July. Our house was burnt the very next day," says Jhorna who was in her third year of graduation back then. As we settled down in her front yard—her house is fully repaired now—a few men and women from the village walked in.

Pleasantries were exchanged. A *bota* of *paan-tamul*[1] was kept on a table in the centre as cups of tea were passed around. They had all survived the outbreak of violence in 2012—all these men and women had lost their homes to the loot and

---

[1] Betel leaves (*paan*) and raw areca nut (*tamul*) served in a brass plate with stands called *bota*

arson and they had all spent some very nervous, edgy days at the refugee camps.

And yet here they were—Zaitoon Khatoon, a Muslim and Protima Basumatary, a Bodo, partaking the *paan-tamul* from the same bowl!

The origin of the violence on 21 July is steeped in mystery. There are various versions—there is one in which first two Muslim men were killed on 19 July, which was followed by the killing of four Bodo Liberation Tigers (BLT) members on 20 July in Kokrajhar. There is another version in which two Muslim student leaders were killed on 4 July and the Bodos retaliated against the Muslims with further killing and arson. In another version, Bodos attacked Muslim youths for the alleged rape and murder of two Bodo girls.

Whatever the genesis of this particular conflict may have been, the violence had spread to Chirang and the real reason for the killings is the manifestation of pressures on land and resources. In a nutshell, the British got the Santhals to work in the tea gardens and later in the mid-1930s, the hardworking cultivators from East Bengal began to arrive for work. The indigenous Bodos, who were also cultivators, were convinced that they were being robbed of their land and found themselves up against the Adivasis and the Muslims.

On the night Jhorna's family of six left their home, there were nearly 66 Bodo families who went to the school at Jaraguri. This school-turned-refugee camp was to become their homes for the next five months. Zaitoon and 169 other families left for the high school in the village; they stayed in the camp for nearly three months.

She insists they aren't refugees. "We have been here forever," says Zaitoon.

The first to come back, Zaitoon spent a night in whatever was left of her house. "The relief camps were crammed and it had rained. Within a few weeks, cases of diarrhoea and malaria became rampant. I wanted to get back home." The next morning she found slogans of 'Bangladeshi go back' painted on her wall. "It was scary. I went to West Bengal which is just a few kilometres from here and stayed at a relative's for a couple of days."

Protima's refugee camp was no better. There was a shortage of food, lack of toilets and diseases were rampant. "The government distributed some clothes but we sold those off so that we could get some money. Almost all our assets were destroyed. We lost our livelihood and livestock."

The conflict disrupted lives on both sides of the divide. Between Kokrajhar and Chirang, there were 164 camps and over 3,00,000 Internally Displaced Persons (IDPs). Oxfam supported 20 IDP camps, 10 in each district.

At the Refugee Camps

"Oxfams have responded to conflict in Assam in the past, however, the programmes were short-term and it was almost 20 years back," recalls Zubin Zaman, humanitarian manager in 2012.

For Oxfam India, it was a first.

"Once we picked our focus states (which included Assam and Uttar Pradesh), there was no way we wouldn't have responded to the conflicts. We had not done it before but we built our skills and expertise in responding to conflicts," says Nisha Agrawal, former CEO of Oxfam India.

These conflicts disrupted lives; if Oxfam had to start responding, it had to make sure it went beyond relief camps and provided livelihood security to those returning home. Something on the lines of the recovery programme after the Kosi floods had to be executed.

The board agreed; they wanted to first visit the camps. Given the sensitivity of the conflict, NGO involvement was carefully assessed by the government. For the initial assessment, a local NGO staff supported the Oxfam team; he had worked with Oxfam during the 2004 floods that had badly affected the district.

Zubin and Bipul Borah (humanitarian programme coordinator) from Oxfam India's humanitarian hub conducted a rapid assessment and reported back a recommendation for immediate response. The programme started, the board members visited and funds flowed in for the conflict.

The conditions of the camps were such that the focus was entirely on WASH. Hand pumps with proper drainage and water storage facilities were installed. IDP camps were crammed with hundreds of people residing in it and with very poor hygiene conditions. There were no sanitation facilities in the camps. Majority of the camps faced a very likely threat of disease outbreak.

Temporary toilets and bathing cubicles were set up. Water filters, buckets to store water and hygiene kits were distributed. The camps were dark, so solar lamps were given as safety measures. As winter was quickly approaching, blankets and tarpaulins were provided. Oxfam was in full swing ensuring the basics to the IDPs who were likely to be in these camps for the next seven to eight months.

Very few aid agencies and NGOs were present at the camp. But Raju Narzary's North East Research & Social Work Networking (NERSWN) was there. A fairly new NGO, they had started volunteering in similar relief camps almost a decade ago. In the initial days, after the violence broke out, Raju and his team were almost the first to go in.

"We hadn't done any relief work. So we were doing some work on a very small-scale like providing vegetables along with some food items, detergent and bleaching powder. So when they came in and started using terms like WASH and Sphere standards, it just went over our heads," he laughs. We were meeting up with him at his NGO campus in Kokrajhar. The campus has a weaving centre and the cloth that is produced by weavers here is sold at a shop in the main market.

"But we learnt a lot." Raju and his team had experience of working with the IDPs in the past and had the expertise to provide psychosocial support. People in these camps go through trauma and they need to be heard, cared for and to an extent distracted, even. "People in these camps are under a lot of stress. We held cultural events, showed films and figured out ways to get children back to school."

They soon realised that these IDPs needed to go back to their homes in their villages—Bodos and Muslims are dependent on each other for their livelihood. "If they stayed back at the relief camp they would continue blaming the other." For Raju, the tipping point was a visit by Praveen Togadia (then with the Vishwa Hindu Parishad) in 2013 to one of the Bodo camps. Known for making inflammatory speeches against Muslims, he made one at the camp painting the ethnic violence in very communal colours.

From Relief Camp to Homes

Zaitoon wanted to get back to her home desperately but what bothered her was the fact that her Bodo neighbours weren't returning yet. When she reached West Bengal, she made some calls to a few Bodo women she was friendly with. She asked them to come back to the village, "We had to start living our lives and staying together like we always did."

Even today she refuses to believe that Bodos set her house on fire. She had hidden with her sister in the banana plantation close to her house when people set her house on fire. "They were not Bodos. There were no Bodos in the village that day."

She and a few other Muslim women used to meet Bodo women at a central place, go to their homes, set it right bit by bit and then go back to the camp at night. And they were able to get back after a few months. While there were individual efforts to build confidence and camaraderie, majority of IDPs lived with palpable fear and mistrust.

They had been on the edge, to begin with! Raju cites an incident. "It was in the beginning of the response. One of my staff, Abdul, went to a Muslim refugee camp. As soon as they knew a Bodo headed his NGO, they beat him up. In that sense, it was good that Oxfam had taken the lead."

"For almost a year, no business happened between the two communities. People were not able to go about their lives and earn their livelihoods," says Abinash Lakhar, programme coordinator of conflict response, who was brought in for the recovery phase of the programme. He has now moved to Delhi with another aid agency.

When he joined, an initial assessment showed that a lot of people, especially Muslims, hadn't received compensation because they didn't have the documents to show that the land they were living on was theirs. That is also because they were actually living on a rich landlord's land and hence had no proof to show. This was particularly difficult for women-led households and single women. Oxfam India and NERSWN stepped in to help with the bureaucratic process.

Those getting back to their villages had to deal with burnt homes and destroyed wells. OIN worked in 20 villages; it first went about making tube wells and toilets. In Chirang, where there was a severe water crisis, Oxfam's tube wells were a godsend. "It was embarrassing how the women kept blessing us for the tube wells," recalls Abinash.

While the tube wells were still there in a few villages in Kokrajhar, the transitional or makeshift toilets were long gone. People had made toilets on their own later.

Then came the paddy and vegetable seeds (to suit the local conditions as recommended by the KVK) and the tiller machines for farming. Goats and piglets were distributed; goats survived, most of the piglets didn't. And it was mostly because of the lack of post-vaccination care. The piglets fetch a lot of money and were hence distributed. Nearly 99 per cent of livestock was distributed to women since they looked after the animals and it was their decision to sell or keep livestock.

The most important of all were the cash transfers—conditional and unconditional. The former was for agriculture purposes and livestock, while the latter was given to the poorest, most vulnerable families for whatever they felt was the priority. As in all recovery programmes, a village committee including the *Gaonbura* (the village headman) would make a list of the most vulnerable based on Oxfam's criteria; the list would then be vetted and finalised. Disabled, single women and women-headed households were given preference.

Between aid agencies such as OIN providing the hardware to put their life in order and NERSWN bringing back normalcy in their lives, people gradually settled back. However, this in no way is the end of a long history of conflict between Bodos, Bengali Muslims and Santhals. The resource squeeze will rear its ugly head sooner than later once again. But the meeting at Jhorna's house showed that Bodos and Bengali Muslims were prepared to give peace a shot.

But things were different in Muzaffarnagar.

Remembering September 2013

It was a fine February afternoon in 2018. Considering it was Muzaffarnagar, perhaps 'quiet' was the more appropriate word. It was still a few days away but the smell of Holi filled the air. We—Gita and Kavita from the NGO called Astitva, and I—were headed to Harsoli village in Muzaffarnagar's Baghara block.

Harsoli, about 20 km from the district headquarters, was one of the villages where scores of Muslim families took refuge from the rioting Hindus on 7 September 2013. As we stopped for tea at a roadside *dhaaba*, Gita walked me through the events that led to the Muzaffarnagar riots—one of the worst in recent times—like she must have done a million times to reporters, aid workers and activists.

An altercation between three boys in Kawal village on 27 August 2013, blew into a full-fledged riot within 10 days. First, the two Hindu boys attacked and killed a Muslim youth who had allegedly eve-teased and misbehaved with their sister. Soon the two were beaten to death by an angry Muslim mob. This triggered inflammatory speeches, a maha panchayat, and a final flare-up on 7 September that spread to Muzaffarnagar and Shamli districts.[2] It didn't take long for the incident to get politicised. Rioting and exodus followed for days. The

[2] Mishra, Ish, Mohan Rao, Pragya Singh and Vikas Bajpai, 'Fact Finding Report: Independent Inquiry into Muzaffarnagar "Riots"', *Economic and Political Weekly*, Vol. 46, No. 2, 2014, https://www.epw.in/journal/2014/2/reports-states-web-exclusives/fact-finding-report-independent-inquiry-muzaffarnagar

government estimate put the death toll at between 48 and 60; over 40,000 people were displaced.

I met Rehana Adib at her first-floor office in Pur Qazi. She is a social activist and heads Astitva. At the time we met, she was still trying to get justice for the women who were raped in the 2013 riots. And in between phone calls, planning projects with her team and shooing away a pigeon that kept flying into the room, she takes my questions.

She explains how 2013 was waiting to happen. There were sporadic incidents of harassment of Muslims—youth, women, men—on the road, on trains, in public transports but they went unreported. Uttar Pradesh had just had elections in 2012 with Samajwadi Party's Akhilesh Yadav taking on the reins of the state and the country was gearing up for national elections in 2014.

"A communal tinderbox, UP, and especially districts like Muzaffarnagar were on very shaky grounds. Cadres of young Hindu men had started to crop up everywhere. We were beginning to hold dialogues and *nukkad nataks* (street plays) to spread communal harmony and peace. Then the incident happened and everything simply hurtled into a riotous situation," Rehana says with a hint of grief, sorrow and anger at how the next few days changed the fabric of the place.

The Budhana-Muzaffarnagar Road is lined with eucalyptus trees, farms, shops, houses, schools, a mosque here, a temple there; a cluster of homes and shops usually mark the entry to a village. The car turned right from the highway towards Harsoli village. As we drove past the bluish-white *pucca* houses on the left and sugarcane fields to the right, the *azaan* went off in a nearby mosque. We left the car behind in one of the streets in the Muslim colony of the village. On the right was the Hindu colony. They didn't mingle. Not anymore.

An occasional car and a bike passed us by. Children, in white *kurta pyjamas* and skull caps, huddled together in front of a shop. They looked at us with equal amounts of suspicion and inquisitiveness. One of the kid said, "*Jai Bajrang Bali, tod dushman ki nali.*" Gita and Kavita were regulars here, they recognised some of the kids. We smiled; they looked at us with a sheepish grin. Perhaps this was their way of acknowledging the presence of Hindus in their midst. They got back to their games, we moved on; we were still a few minutes away from Nayi Basti.

The Horror of Muzaffarnagar

Nayi Basti is one of the refugee camps where Muslim families took refuge to escape the rioting in their villages. Families settled here are mostly those who escaped from Dindawali village close to Kutbi-Kutba and Kawal, the epicentre of the riot. The camp, at the end of the village nestled between a *masjid* and sugarcane fields, has now become a colony in Harsoli village; it has an overhead water tank, a mix of semi-*pucca* and *kachcha* houses and a toilet outside every house.

The refugee colony mostly has women, children and older men; young men have migrated. They earlier worked as labourers in the farms of the Hindus—that option no longer exists. Most lost their tools and implements while fleeing their homes. So those who didn't lose their lives lost their livelihoods. Back in 2013, men who had already migrated and were nowhere close to Muzaffarnagar were perhaps the luckiest. They lived. They came back only after a few days, once the rioting stopped, to either bury the dead or to find their families alive but homeless in different campsites.

Women we meet at Nayi Basti recall the events of 7 September as though it had just happened yesterday. "Announcements were made from the mosques warning the villagers. The Hindus had assembled in temples and schools with swords and guns. We were completely unarmed and unprepared; Hindus, on the other hand, had been planning it for a few days"; "We started leaving latching on to lorries, *jugaads*, any mode of transport we could lay our hands on to go to safer villages, to relatives and friends"; "Some of us left on foot. We walked through fields, alongside water canals to keep out of the way of the rioters. We always moved in groups. We kept walking through the night to reach a safer place."

They were the lucky ones who survived. The women continue—men were rounded up and killed or maimed; women were beaten up, raped and gang-raped; children and the elderly tied up and burnt. They recall how infants were buried with calves in a pile of cow dung cakes and set on fire.

Young girls continued to be victims even after the riots. Concerns about 'family honour' and fear of further violence resulted in a large number of underage girls, especially those in relief camps, being married off. In fact, religious leaders promoted marriage as a solution rather than ensuring security and the state announced financial assistance for the same though it was later withdrawn. An Astitva report states that at least 398 marriages had taken place.

To escape trigger-crazed rioters, women and children hid in large grain storage containers only to be later rescued by the CRPF. Not far from Nayi Basti, lives Shabnam* in a refugee camp-turned-colony at Parsoli village. She recalls the horror when she and her child hid under a pile of wood to escape the mob. She had cupped her child's mouth so tight, to stop her from crying, that she didn't even realise that the child wasn't crying or breathing. Her eyes had rolled up and were vacant. She only remembers clutching the child close to her chest and crying. "My child survived. It was a miracle."

But Salma* wasn't so lucky. She had wrapped her newborn in a blanket and was escaping on foot. Clutching the blanket tightly, she reached one of the campsites only to find that the baby had slipped out of the blanket at some point. Tears well up as she recounts the incident. Her child would have been five this year.

Houses were razed; in many cases, the elderly refused to leave their homes; sixty-year-old Hasmati* locked herself up in her ancestral home and spent days holed up in there. Mosques were desecrated and ripped apart. What made matters worse was the fact that the rioters and pillagers weren't strangers; these young Hindu men were acquaintances, employers, landlords and some were very good friends who had turned enemies overnight.

---

* Name changed.

Lives were lost on both sides, but the numbers were skewed against the Muslims. Reports and fact-finding teams, along with victim testimonies show that the police turned a blind eye and let the riots flare up. Political apathy was evident. Bureaucrats at the helm of affairs were in and out of offices; government relief work was at best missing.

Religious organisations like the Jamiat Ulema-e-Hind of Deoband swung into action; fact-finding reports show that the state, in fact, chose to outsource relief work to these Islamic organisations. They provided shelter in the refugee camps, which have now turned into colonies—Falah-e-Aam Colony in Parsoli village came upon land given by the mosques and *madrasas*. There were others, which were set up on forestland or in sugarcane fields and they had to be vacated within a few months.

Wading Through Uncharted Territory

Oxfam India had responded to conflicts in the past, but nothing like this—politically charged and communal. Moreover, when the riots broke out, the team was already responding (early recovery and restoration) to the Bodo-Muslim conflict in Assam (from 2012) and Uttarakhand floods (from June 2013). Later they would also get busy in responding to Cyclone Phailin in October.

"It took time to assess the full impact of the violence, and information from the ground was sketchy. The incidents started in August and sporadic violence continued up to September. During these two months, the situation was extremely volatile," says Zubin. They swung into action after the board took a considered decision that Oxfam India should respond.

As soon as they got the nod, they went through the routine of risk analysis, assessment, intervention requirements and relationships with different stakeholders. The assessment was completed on 5 October, the proposal was sent to ECHO (European Civil Protection and Humanitarian Aid Operations) and funds came in enough for them to stay from October to March. Some funding also came from Christian Aid.

"These funds were important. In communal riots, few aid agencies go in and fewer stay back for a long period of time. There is always a fear of political backlash. And unlike natural disasters, raising funds for responding to communal riots is extremely challenging. We managed to get funds because the kind of intervention we planned was more…hardware," says Zubin. He moved on from Oxfam India to join Oxfam International's Global Humanitarian Team in 2016.

During the six-month response, Oxfam India reached out to over 24,000 people in 10 camps both at Muzaffarnagar and Shamli.

Funding in place, the next hurdle was perception. "The camp was frequented by political and religious leaders and they were always asking what our 'agenda' was, what our 'intent' was. They wouldn't believe that we were there for purely humanitarian reasons," says Zubin.

It had thus become very important that Oxfam India did not look biased or political. "We were following a code of conduct that 'we do not discriminate against anyone'. So we decided to first meet with both communities in the camp, that is, Hindus and Muslims. It turned out that these camps only had Muslims. Displacement among the Hindus was negligible. We were going to help everyone and anyone who was there in the 10 camps in Shamli and Muzaffarnagar."

These camps were run by religious organisations such as the Jamiat Ulema-e-Hind with the full backing of the *madrasas* and the mosques. The communal nature of the riots meant that aid agencies were under the scanner of the clerics and the police.

Oxfam always responds alongside local partners. This ensures ease of access and a better understanding of the situation at hand. And so Rehana's NGO, Astitva, came on board. Their experience of working in the district and with the community made them the obvious choice for a partnership. Just like Oxfam India, this was their first communal riot response too. Rehana and her team were working in Muzaffarnagar on issues of violence against women, which included both Muslims and Hindus.

"Once the riot broke, we held discussions in office and it was decided that we should go and reach out to women and families who have been affected—both Muslim and Hindu. Over the next few days, we divided ourselves and went to practically all the camps in the two districts," recalls Rehana. Astitva had already visited the camps, assessed the situation and tried to provide food and medicines. They made a list of IDPs in the different camps which came in handy for Oxfam's response.

"They were a very strong group of women who worked on gender. However, it would have been challenging for a local NGO to implement the programme alone, given the complexity of the programme, external relations and donor compliance. Oxfam took the lead in responding to the crisis with the partner providing support on community mobilisation for programme activities in the IDP camps. As a humanitarian actor, working on humanitarian principles of impartiality, neutrality and independence, Oxfam was well accepted by the community," says Zubin.

By leadership, he means, taking the lead in talking to the authorities or the clerics and other stakeholders. Holding coordination meetings and sharing regular information and feedback with the administration helped them to smoothly continue providing assistance to the affected IDPs. The relationship also helped Oxfam India and Astitva, to approach government officials for support when challenges cropped up in the programme.

Further elaborating on the risk assessment, he talks of the other decision that was taken. Oxfam India located its field base in Roorkee; the ground situations were challenging and options of operating from Muzaffarnagar were risky given the continued tension and violence in the conflict-affected areas. Information was shared daily between partners and Oxfam staff, which helped to plan and implement the programme as per schedule. This was to ensure that the team could assess risks regularly and mitigate them.

This response was complex and challenging. Oxfam India deployed its technical staff, which comprised water and sanitation technicians, livelihood specialists, and finance and logistics personnel. "While there was a general acceptance of staff that were deployed from other programme locations, we had to be careful in getting the right staff for the programme," he says.

It is in this context of the complex humanitarian crisis in Muzaffarnagar that Oxfam India began to establish its presence in the IDP camps and built its relationship with the community which helped in ensuring that the response programme was unhindered and could continue to address the vital needs of the affected population.

At the Relief Camps

By October, the team hit the ground running. The warehouse was in place and supplies were brought in. Beneficiary cards were distributed, based on the primary list that Astitva prepared and after some due diligence on the part of the hub. The card was a way to ensure that there was no duplication and that no one that Oxfam India-Astitva had identified was left behind.

Oxfam set up shelters in the camps, built hand pumps with aprons, constructed privacy cabins for women to bathe in and set up latrines in the camp. They distributed tarpaulin; two blankets and EP foam sheets for insulation and bedding support in temporary shelters; smokeless cook stoves; and solar lamps. A WASH kit—soaps, a bucket and a mug—along with combs, nail cutters and material for sanitary napkins were provided.

Many at the Falah-e-Aam Colony still had their beneficiary card and the solar lamps!

These camps were likely to stay for some time and with no drainage, clean drinking water, cooking space, toilets or bathing space, the camps were extremely vulnerable to a disease outbreak. WASH trainings were given, WASH committees were formed and hygiene activities were aggressively implemented to mitigate the public health risks and threats.

A dear friend working with Amnesty once pointed out that Oxfam's intervention with the shelter and WASH kits were a blessing, especially since they had lost everything and the government's relief and response were missing!

Apart from supporting Oxfam, Astitva had also started helping those in the campsites with approaching the police and filing FIRs. Oxfam's protection interventions were moderate and focused on addressing the immediate support that IDPs would need, particularly women and adolescent girls. This involved the provision of solar lamps for lighting and also ensuring that they had safe access to toilets. Astitva provided the more substantive protection interventions, given their presence in the district, and protection interventions being a part of their organisational mandate.

"Women and children were in trauma. We decided we would spend time with these women and help them out of the shock," says Rani, a colleague of Rehana's. But the refugee camp and stories of loss, abuse, rape and cold-blooded murder got to Rehana's team of young women and men.

We were still with the survivors and listening to their heart-rending stories at the Falah-e-Aam colony when Rani recalled how volunteers would break down while talking about their daily visits. "My father always encouraged me to do this work. But these stories disturbed him to the extent that his health started failing. He passed away during the response," Rani says. But she continued working.

So Rehana had on her hands the task of assuaging frayed nerves of not just those who were struggling in the camps but also her own volunteers and staff.

Starting from Scratch

"They asked me to come back to the village and teach. But they also say they cannot guarantee my safety," said a *maulvi* I had met at one of the camps. We met him at the house of one of the survivors. By 'they' he means the Hindus. "How can anyone go back without any assurance?"

The initial response to the conflict was completed by March 2014; the recovery programme—to rehabilitate livelihoods—began soon after that. In those months, it had become very clear that the refugee camps were going to become their permanent homes. There was nothing for them to go back to. Their houses were looted and burned down. They were not welcome in the village any more—Muslim families had been driven away. Their children could no longer go to the schools in those villages. Mosques and *kabrastans* (graveyards) had been vandalised.

Their livelihood had been taken away—they could no longer work in the sugarcane fields or as masons or *mistry*. Those who had flourishing local businesses were left with nothing and had to resort to daily wage labour. Men and women could not take up work offered under the National Rural Employment Guarantee Act (NREGA) for fear of recurring violence.

The government promised compensation—a few got them, a few are still fighting to get them, many lost hope. So if any work had to be done in this phase, it would have to be for those who got no compensation, who were left with a disability, women-led families and women.

Men had migrated again to rebuild their lives. Just this time, they left families in refugee camps. Meanwhile, Oxfam's Lucknow office was contemplating working with Muslims, given their large numbers in the state. Muzaffarnagar became the obvious choice. "The concern there was to bring about social harmony, build their trust as well as address the massive loss of livelihood of the displaced as a result of the riots," says Nand Kishore Singh, the regional manager of Lucknow.

Discussions were held with those at the camps. They wanted to simply regain their means of livelihood. But they weren't sure what or how. They were working as farm labourers earlier or as carpenters and *mistry* in the village; these options were unavailable.

Goatery and poultry were promoted. Masons, barbers, carpenters and blacksmiths who had lost their implements were supported with toolkits. Given the sugarcane belt, men were trained to make jaggery and sell it. "We tried to link them to the markets in whatever they were doing so that their chances of livelihood improved," explains Nand Kishore Singh.

Women were trained to use sewing machines; sewing centres were set up and a network established with local industries to ensure a regular stream of income. *Hunarshalas* or *Hunar Ghars* were set up. These were on the lines of an experiment done in Lucknow, where women artisans doing *zardosi* work were given a place to come together, discuss, share problems and work. This concept seemed particularly useful after the riots as this would help rebuild trust and give a sense of community to the women who were living under the shadow of fear.

Apart from Oxfam India and Astitva, there were others such as Afkar India Foundation and Centre for Equity Studies (CES) who were working with the survivors on different aspects at the refugee camps. Survivors still needed justice, they needed compensation and access to government schemes and they needed harmony and peace in their lives. But given the political environment and the clampdown on civil society, this wouldn't have been possible by one organisation. So an alliance of aid agencies and local and national civil society organisations was built—Muzaffarnagar Adhikar Jan Manch Alliance (MAJMA).

Oxfam too was a part of it. Just as they had worked doggedly and still kept a low profile at the relief camps, so they backed the alliance and their fight to get the survivors justice. Silently, and with all its heart!

"They are farmers and farmworkers, horticulturists and market sellers, businesswomen and community leaders. Rural women are the backbone of sustainable livelihoods and provide food security for their families and communities."

—**UN Secretary-General Ban Ki-moon's** message
on the International Day of Rural Women
15 October 2015

Women Farmers and Their Land Rights
Aaroh Campaign
2006–17
Uttar Pradesh

The premise of the project was simple—women do most of the work in the farm and yet have no legal rights over land, resources or schemes. They are not even recognised as farmers. The women farmers themselves do not consider themselves as farmers. For them, what they are doing is part of the chores!

A study by FAO shows that if women have equal access to land as men, agriculture productivity of developing countries will increase by 20–30 per cent and this would have the potential to reduce malnutrition by 12–17 per cent.

Despite the positives, the land ownership of women is abysmally low—only 12.69 per cent of women in rural India have operational land ownership, including leased land (2010–11 agriculture census). This is lower than some of the poorer African countries like Zambia (17 per cent) and Malawi (32 per cent).

The demand for women's land rights is not a new phenomenon. In the Bodhgaya movement (a farmers movement in Bihar), women farmers participated in large numbers and demanded land rights. The Centre and the states have, over the years, tried to promote women's land ownership with a slew of legislations such as the amendment to the Hindu Succession Act in 2005, joint titles, lower registration fee and land to the landless. Yet these have failed to make an impact on land ownership. Patriarchal mindset and deep-set regressive social norms have kept women from demanding their rights over land and property.

It was this vicious cycle that Aaroh Campaign was trying to break. Aaroh Campaign emerged as a movement that harnessed the power of women farmers across the state;

their relentless campaigning for their demands and social acceptance bore fruit when 15 October was declared as National Women Farmer's Day. Aaroh Campaign brought to the fore firebrand leaders.

This is the story of these women.

We Are the Women Farmers

Tractor Lady and Cyclewali

Sabita Parida and I reached Saharanpur, in Western Uttar Pradesh, to meet the women farmers. The drive was smooth barring the last stretch of dusty, bumpy and narrow roads. After a quick stopover at Disha's office (an NGO based in Saharanpur), we headed to Patni village. Women farmers had already assembled on the terrace of a house where the meeting was to be held. A few trickled in as we were doing our rounds of introductions. With the introductions out of the way, the meeting had begun. Or so, I thought.

Sabita was taking out her notebook and I was still rehearsing the opening lines for the meeting in my head when the women broke into one of their rallying cries:

"महिला भी किसान है, ये ही देश की शान है।"

("*Women are farmers too, we are the pride of the country.*")

The meeting had *now* begun.

This was in 2015. This more or less summed up the sentiment and laid out the agenda for this meeting and all other subsequent meetings in Shahjahanpur, Pilibhit, Gorakhpur, Ambedkar Nagar, Faizabad and Sant Kabir Nagar. We were travelling to meet with women farmers who were part of the Aaroh Campaign. Sabita, then a programme coordinator, was overseeing this project since 2011. While she was familiar with the women, I was meeting them for the first time.

I was meeting Suresho, who goes by the sobriquet 'Tractor Lady' for being the only woman who drove a tractor back then. She wrestled her piece of land from her in-laws. She, in fact, inspired her father-in-law who gave his other daughter-in-law her share as well. She began farming on her land. An active member of the Aaroh Mahila Kisaan Manch, she cultivates her own land, supports her natal family and has enrolled her son in an English-medium school.

For the first time, I was meeting the sixty-year-old *cyclewali*, Leelawati. She is called *cyclewali* because she goes to the *mandi* to sell vegetables on her cycle. She has bought land in the name of her daughters-in-law, grows organic vegetables on her land and is a member of the Agriculture Technology Management Agency (ATMA) board. She has the number of the agriculture officer on speed dial who she calls up anytime she suspects a pest attack in her farm.

For the first time, I was meeting Manju Tiwari. She got her husband's land registered in her name when she suspected him of planning to sell off their land and elope with a younger girl. He did elope. The girl's family filed a false complaint against her; she evaded arrest with the help of the Aaroh Mahila Kisaan Manch, found her absconding husband, got him arrested and got on with her life. She farms and takes care of her three children.

And the list goes on.

These women were in control of their lives and their livelihoods. Through the Aaroh Campaign that ran from 2006 to 2017, they began to be recognised as farmers. It took several marches, sit-ins, *gheraos*, in-your-face campaigning and petitions before the media, the government, the agriculture department and even the men in their families and society acknowledged them as farmers.

The dogged campaigning around the identity of women farmers finally bore fruit in 2016. The Ministry of Agriculture and Farmers Welfare declared 15 October as *Mahila Kisaan Divas*.[1] This was a sweet victory for two reasons. One, the campaign had been demanding for 15 October—International Rural Women's Day—to be dedicated to women farmers. Two, though the campaign had been successful in making dents within the state, this government order gave it a stamp of approval from the Centre.

Farmer no longer meant only man. The campaign had come a long way.

The Mahanagar Meeting in 2005

Having worked with small, marginal and landless farmers in various parts of Uttar Pradesh, Dr Shiraz A Wajih, president of the Gorakhpur Environmental Action Group (GEAG) was amazed by the fact that women farmers in Gorakhpur, despite doing most of the work in the farm, were financially backward. Men had migrated and it was incumbent on the women to continue farming but they were unable to access credit facilities or inputs from the agriculture department because the land that they farmed on was not in their name. They were not landowners and so, they were not recognised as farmers.

Dr Wajih, then a partner of Oxfam Great Britain (OGB), called a meeting of like-minded NGOs in Lucknow; few were already associated with Oxfam, others not. Bharat Bhushan

[1] http://pib.nic.in/newsite/PrintRelease.aspx?relid=171730 (as viewed on 16 May 2018).

of PANI Sansthan, a Faizabad-based NGO, recalls, "We were nearly 15 of us. We held our first meeting in a small room in Mahanagar in Lucknow. The premise was simple—something needed to be done to get women their rights and their recognition as farmers." Kanchan Sinha, who headed Oxfam's North India office, was also present at that meeting.

Most of these NGOs were working on issues of women's livelihood and empowerment, working on their identity and rights as a farmer was still uncharted territory. Discussions continued for nearly a year. "We were used to working in a project mode. But many discussions later, and encouraged by Kanchan ji, we decided that this had to be done in a campaign mode," recalls Bhushan.

Kanchan was associated with Oxfam for nearly two decades; her last stint was as the country head of Tanzania between 2008 and 2010. She was instrumental in shaping the campaign, thus, meeting Kanchan was imperative. We met in May in Oxfam's Lucknow office. She walked me through the thinking behind the project, what it set out to achieve and how it was envisaged.

Campaign mode, she explains, didn't mean campaign really. "It just meant that it had to be a continuous process and not just activity-based." The problem was in front of them and they started to identify the goal. "At the end, women will have rights over their land and resources, they will be recognised as farmers and they will have all the capacities of a good farmer. They will also be able to take their produce to the market, keep their own profits and use it accordingly. This was the end goal. We had to understand where we were on these issues and where we had to start."

There is a barometer to understand why someone is marginalised and the project should be designed to address these, she explains. Lack of access to economic resources, lack of capacities (good health, good education, information, exposure), lack of choice and options, and finally, lack of basic citizenship rights (human rights) are the four criteria, she points out too.

"These are interlinked issues. In the case of women farmers, if you look at giving them recognition, you will have to look at the whole spectrum—of getting their rights as farmers socially to getting the government to give them their rights as farmers. This was a long path to be traversed. And we had to start somewhere." So Kanchan's idea was to go with the low hanging fruit—the more solvable ones first before moving to the next challenge.

The Aaroh Campaign is clearly built on the framework Kanchan suggested. And perhaps this is the reason they went step by step, going after the low hanging fruits and making one dent at a time. The project was broadly divided into two phases. First, take the information to women farmers—information about land, prevalent laws and extension services. Second, a target was set to get joint ownership of land for men and women and ensure the rights of women as farmers.

For the project, Uttar Pradesh was divided into five regions—Western, North-Western (Rohilkhand), Central, Eastern and the Bundelkhand regions. Each region, with 10 districts, was headed by one NGO each—Disha Samajik

Sansthan, Vinobha Seva Ashram, PANI Sansthan, GEAG and Samarpan Jan Kalyan Samiti, respectively. They were part of the discussions from the very beginning and thus, became the natural partners and leaders of Aaroh Campaign.[2]

At the time of drawing the blueprint of the project, it became clear that there wasn't enough data on women's participation in farming, their land ownership, access to institutional credit or government schemes. Numbers were needed. So in 2006, a survey of 2,500 households was carried out to get some clarity on the missing data.

The Numbers Were Dismal

सौ में सत्तर काम हमारे, लिखो बही में नाम हमारे।

(*We do 70 out of 100 jobs in agriculture, include our names in the land deed.*)

Only 6.5 per cent women owned land, and these were either widows (81 per cent) or single children (19 per cent); only 3 per cent women had joint titles, nearly 87 per cent had no land rights; 4.2 per cent women could take a decision on what to sow, 28.4 per cent women could decide when and what to sell; 8 per cent had control over the agriculture income; only 2 per cent women had access to credit; and, 1 per cent to agriculture extension services.

---

[2] With a solid footing in the regions, all these NGOs had the solid backing of many smaller grassroots organisations and this really took the campaign far and wide. GEAG became the secretariat for the campaign. The campaign started with 50 districts but it eventually ended with 70 (owing to the subsequent division of some of these districts).

True to Dr Shiraz's observation, women were the labourers in their fields without any rights. The numbers were dismal!

Despite a dash of pro-women policy[3] corrections, the complete lack of acceptance of women as farmers by the government, prevailing social norms, patriarchy and discrimination of women meant that the Act was never used to its full potential.[4] UPZALR and other land legislations were repealed in 2012 and replaced by one comprehensive law—the Uttar Pradesh Revenue Code, 2006. The Hindu Succession Amendment Act, 2005, which gives property rights to daughters, is not applicable to agricultural land in Uttar Pradesh.

In fact, while the Revenue Code Bill was being finalised, the women farmers of Aaroh Campaign advocated for rights over land for women. They met with the governor. "He said the demand was too big. But he assured us he would consider our demands," says Neelam Prabhat, the lead campaigner for Aaroh. The amendment of the Revenue Code Bill included

[3] Historically, there were a few attempts to improve the socio-economic status of women in the state. In 1995, the Uttar Pradesh State Revenue Department issued an order under Section 126 of the Uttar Pradesh Zamindari Abolition and Land Reforms (UPZALR) Act to issue land titles or *pattas* for agricultural land jointly in the name of the husband and wife. Further, it amended to add that sole titles to land would be given to 'unmarried but adult daughters whose parents are no longer alive, and to abandoned and widowed women who are landless agricultural labourers'.

[4] Kelkar, Govind and Santosh Kumar Jha, 'Women's Agential Power in the Political Economy of Agricultural Land', *Agrarian South: Journal of Political Economy* 5, No. 1, 2016, pp. 98–122.

'wife' in the definition of a family. This meant she would have a say in the sale of land. This was a small but crucial win.

And Thus Began the Aaroh Campaign

Aaroh means ascent or moving ahead. This campaign was the *aaroh* of women farmers.

Neelam was brought on board as the campaign lead in March 2006. In the first few weeks, she travelled across the state to identify coordinators for the different regions; five coordinators were selected. Around this time, a Steering Committee was formed to strategise, shape and guide the campaign.

"The first meeting of the committee was held on 18 April 2006. This was very symbolic. This was the day the Bhoodan Movement had started in 1951," recalls Neelam. This meeting was held to sharpen the finer logistical features of the campaign and strategy to work with women farmers.

I had first met Neelam in Gorakhpur in 2015. I was meeting her again in April 2018, this time at her Lucknow home. She had greyed a little more; the orange streaks of *mehendi* had increased. We discussed Aaroh over the din of a loudspeaker blaring devotional songs, just outside her house. She was battling migraine the day I met her. It triggered if she stayed out in the sun even for a little while, she explains. "This never happened when I was with the campaign. I used to travel a lot, hold a lot of meetings. Every three months, we used to have regional meetings. But apart from that, I would attend at least some of the monthly Manch meetings somewhere in the state. I was perpetually on the move," she smiles.

Neelam often jumps timelines to recall events.

On 15 October 2006, a big meeting was held in Lucknow. The final survey was yet to come in. "Some of the results were in. We wanted to introduce Aaroh Campaign and float the idea of women farmers." Nearly 250 people—bureaucrats, grassroots organisations, academicians, civil society members and the media—attended the meeting. It was well-received.

Neelam loves this date. And not just for the fact that it is observed as the International Rural Women's Day. In December 2016, the Ministry of Agriculture and Farmers Welfare (MoA&FW) declared 15 October as National Women Farmer's Day too.

"There was a lot of campaigning around this, especially from 2012 onwards. This announcement reinforced our demand for recognition of women as farmers. Letters were sent to MPs and MLAs. We had almost sent a letter to the UN with over 10,000 signatures demanding the same." The very mention of these events brings instant joy.

Aaroh Campaign was formally launched with the release of the study on 4 December 2006. It was launched in different districts across the state, on the same date. "This made a huge impact. The coverage was big and dense. The launch was noticed," recalls Neelam.

As she talks about the project, the joy is palpable. And this is true for every woman who was part of the Aaroh Campaign. And they all jump timelines!

Like Leelawati, PANI's project coordinator (and not *cyclewali*), who while talking about her journey switches to the first *padyatra* in January 2007. "It was a sea of women. Nearly 43,000 women joined across the state. There were women driving tractors and bullock carts. Not a single man participated in the *padyatra* but they had all lined up to see what was going on. The entire stretch was lined with inquisitive men. We intrigued them. They wanted to know what women were trying to do. Who were we? What did we want?"

The march made an impact. It got everyone talking about women, about Aaroh, about Aaroh Mahila Kisaan Manch. It would take a few more years, a few more *padyatras*, catchy slogans, public hearings and petitions before everyone would talk about *Mahila Kisaan*.

The Making of Women Farmers

महिला कृषक, किसान या सहयोगी।
(*Women farmers, farmer or helper.*)

First, the women themselves had to believe that they were farmers. "They believed that they were supposed to do all the work they did in their farms. They believed they were labourers. The first few years were spent in socialising the idea that women engaged in farming activities were indeed farmers and Aaroh was going to give them that recognition," says Neelam.

The tone and tenor of women certainly did change. During our 2015 visit, *cyclewali* Leelawati said, "We do all the work in the field. If we don't, men will not be able to farm on their own. So why aren't we farmers?"

Cyclewali Leelawati became the first woman farmer in the state to be awarded the *Kisaan Samman* in 2014.

Women had been felicitated in the past too but it was for allied activities such as animal husbandry, dairy and poultry. Leelawati's award, given only to men until then, was the acknowledgement and acceptance of women as farmers. Prior to the *Kisaan Samman*, at a meeting organised by Oxfam, agricultural scientist MS Swaminathan felicitated three women of the Aaroh Mahila Kisaan Manch in 2012, for their contribution to food production. The awards have not stopped coming since!

The Aaroh Mahila Kisaan Manch rose from the Self-Help Groups (SHGs) that the five main partner NGOs along with their grassroots organisations had built over the years. While it was easy to form the Manch there was a hitch. SHGs were not seen as a threat to the society, they were groups of women involved in saving and lending money. The Manch, on the other hand, was talking about rights of women farmers. This was a sticky issue, perceived as a potential threat to patriarchy. Men stopped their wives from attending these meetings, sometimes violently. Women were beaten up at home and yet they came for the meetings.

To allay their doubts and apprehensions, men were invited to these meetings as well. Women were the focus but men had to become a part of this movement—whether it was for accepting women as farmers or for demanding joint land titles. In one of the years, men were taken along for the annual meeting of the women farmers in Lucknow. It was an eye-opener for them—their women talking with such grit and confidence. "They were assured that women weren't going 'wayward'. They meant business," smiles Bhushan.

These joint sessions dispelled the belief that women were being disruptive, on the contrary, it made them realise that women were not labourers but farmers. That they were equal and that giving them equal rights would boost their household income especially when they migrated.

For women, it was a different experience. Shanti Devi of Ambedkar Nagar explains, "The SHGs were restricted to collecting and managing money. The Manch made us aware of our status as farmers. We also realised that only our husbands had rights. The land was in his name. It was his photo that was on the deed. And because of this, we were not able to benefit from the schemes. Why weren't we being treated as equals?"

हम हैं भूमिजा; हम हैं शैलजा।
हमको नहीं किसान का दर्जा।

(*We are the daughters of the land; we are the daughters of the mountain. Yet we don't have the status of a farmer.*)

The Manch held monthly meetings. The regional meetings were held every quarter.

The campaign was taking one baby step at a time. All the joint meetings were fine, but it was the *Hal Nikaalo* (a march held to claim the plough) Campaign that made a massive impact. After the 2007 *padyatra*, which was spread over 585 gram panchayats across 50 districts, Leelawati recalls, men coming out in support of women farmers.

"Perhaps they couldn't wipe out the image of women driving tractors," laughs Leelawati.

This was a show of power. And it shattered some deep-rooted social norms. The *Hal Nikaalo* Campaign, nearly six years after the first *padyatra*, challenged the norm that women are not supposed to plough. Like the genesis of Aaroh, the *Hal Nikaalo* Campaign had very organic beginnings. When the whole village opposed Lalla Devi tooth and nail for ploughing her field, the Manch rallied around her till it became acceptable.

Lalla Devi, a Dalit, had lost her husband. He was a migrant labourer. Widowed with three children, Lalla was left with some land and oxen. When she decided to plough the field, the entire village opposed and ostracised her on account of an old tradition that forbade women to plough; a plough is seen as a potent symbol of male farmers.

With the backing of the Manch, Lalla stood by her decision. In fact, she went ahead and trained others in the village too. A *fatwa* was issued against one of her trainees. "The *fatwa* meant nothing for these women," laughs Leelawati. Nearly 1.10 lakh women participated in the *Hal Nikaalo* Campaign across the state in 2013–14.

On one occasion, when the sub-divisional magistrate commented on how 'shameful' it was for women to plough the field, Aisha Khatoon called him out. Women farmers present there were furious. "I remember them telling the officer, 'stealing is shameful. This is hard work and nothing to be ashamed of'. SDM *sahib* had to apologise," says Leelawati.

On yet another occasion, during a farmers' meeting with the state agriculture minister in Lucknow, women farmers (from Gorakhpur and Ambedkar Nagar) seated behind shouted, "मिनिस्टर साहब, आप अपनी ही सुनाएंगे या हमारी भी सुनेगें" ("*Mr Minister will you keep talking or will you listen to us also*"). Neelam remembers the minister being taken aback. He apologised for not having realised that they were women farmers. "The members of the Manch complained that they received last-minute invitations for meetings from the district magistrate's office. It didn't matter to the officers that they were unable to attend the meetings. They demanded to be informed in advance and their presence to be mandated for completing the quorum. The minister promised to take appropriate steps."

These women were on a roll!

These were still early days and *Mahila Kisaan*—both as a term and as a concept—was yet to become a part of the administrative lingo.

हम देश के सबल किसान; मेरी भी करो पहचान।

(*We are the able farmers; give us our recognition.*)

The *padyatras* made the agriculture department and media sit up and take note; the strategy to hold events on the same day throughout the state paid dividends. Newspapers were flush with articles on *Mahila Kisaan*. The term was beginning to gain currency and so was their identity.

They became members of *kisaan* clubs[5]—an all-male bastion. As Suresho pointed out (in 2015), 13 women farmers were part of the 25-member *kisaan* club in Saharanpur. The glass ceiling was being shattered, slowly but steadily. They were

---

[5] *Kisaan* clubs or farmer clubs are informal grassroots level forum for farmers, supported by KVKs, rural branches of banks and NGOs; NABARD provides financial assistance to these clubs which are mutually beneficial to the farmers and the banks.

invited as panel speakers on agricultural talk shows telecast on Doordarshan. *Mahila Kisaan* became board members of ATMA. Earlier, the ATMA board, apart from the district collector and district level officials from the agricultural, veterinary and fisheries department, had farmers. But these farmers were never women.

Their inclusion in the board in 2007–08 was a huge step towards recognising them as farmers. By 2017, 32 *Mahila Kisaan* from 23 districts were on the ATMA board. They weren't there to complete a quorum; they were there on the board as decision-makers and a crucial link between the farmers and the officials.

"Earlier we had to go to enquire about the schemes, now they come to us with the information," says Chandravati of Sant Kabir Nagar district. Her Manch, like others across the state, have been able to approach the agriculture department and get for themselves a tractor, a pump set, fencing for the fields and agricultural inputs like seeds, fertilisers and pesticides.

The power equations were changing.

Breaking from general practice, the agriculture department identified women farmers for exposure visits to agriculture universities for training—they were sent to Indian Agricultural Research Institute (IARI), New Delhi and the GB Pant University of Agriculture and Technology, Pantnagar. Women were farming earlier, now they were farming smarter—multi-cropping, layered cropping and vermicomposting (saving on the fertiliser cost). They made the most of it.

Ramkali, a septuagenarian, learnt mushroom farming during one of her Pantnagar visits. Inspired by the yield and returns, she negotiated for a fixed rate for her mushrooms at the Khatima *mandi* in Pilibhit, and in 2015 (when we met her), she was planning to go back to Pantnagar for more mushroom seeds.

It wasn't that they would walk in to these trainings and no one would bat an eyelid. During a training of farmers by the State Agriculture Department, some of the men present asked Durgesh, a woman farmer, to go and join the session on pickle making. "They told her, 'What will you do here?'. She came back disappointed the first day. We asked her to go back. She went and when the men once again tried to push her away, she said, 'I am a farmer. I am here for training of farmers. I will sit here.' And she attended the complete workshop," smiles Leelawati.

They have improved the nutrition of their families and amped their incomes. Most of them have gone pesticide-free. Veerawati puts up a *keetnashak-mukt* board at the *mandi* and it fetches her a premium and some loyal customers. "We keep some aside for ourselves. This has ensured that we get to eat all kinds of seasonal vegetables," she smiles. Traditionally, it was the men who went to the *mandi* barring a few examples like Leelawati. Emboldened by the campaign and the Manch, women farmers too started going to the *mandi*.

From Recognition to Rights

खेत में खलिहान में; फिर क्यों नहीं विधान में।

(*In the farm and the field; why not in the law?*)

Association with the Manch and the subsequent exposure visits to agriculture institutes and other districts marches, and meetings increased the mobility and confidence of women farmers. They began demanding their rights. It was no longer just about social recognition; it was about legal rights. This was the next step and it came with mixed results.

Seher-ul-Nisa landed at the DM office, with her 12 children and other members of the Manch in tow, and demanded that the DM ensure that her husband doesn't sell their land to feed his gambling and drinking habit. The Faizabad DM issued a Government Order (GO) making the wife a co-signatory in case of a land sale. But this couldn't be replicated in other districts; for instance, the Kushinagar DM passed an executive order on similar lines, but it was challenged in court and the order was stayed. However, the 2008 Faizabad GO is applicable even today.

भेजा संदेशा सरकार को; 171 पर विचार हो।

(*Have sent message to the government; reconsider section 171.*)

The following year, the campaign began advocating for joint titles. Though joint titles do not rock the boat, as much as land rights activists would have liked to, it would be a leap demanding for individual titles for women farmers just yet. Women across the state, shared how in the beginning, the officials told them, "Why do you bother? You will get the land after your husband dies." "We asked them, 'Should we start wishing to be widowed just to get what is rightfully ours?'"

Section 171, of the now-repealed UPZALR, stated that the wife (along with a male descendant) gets property/land rights only after the demise of her husband. The surviving male heir too would share this. Aaroh Campaign rallied to make amends to this section along with the demands for joint land rights.

The idea of joint land titles appealed to women for obvious reasons. One, as the Faizabad example showed, men would not be able to sell land without the consent of the wife. Anecdotal evidence established a drastic fall in the sale of land after the GO was issued. And two, when the husbands migrated or, like in Manju's case, in jail, the joint title and subsequently, the *Kisaan* Credit Card (KCC) (given to landowners) would mean that they could avail institutional credit and inputs to improve farm productivity.

Land ownership was mandatory to get the card. The National Commission of Farmer (NCF) constituted in 2006 under the chairmanship of MS Swaminathan recommended that KCC should be issued in the name of women farmers and that joint titles/*pattas* should be used as collateral.[6] Aaroh Campaign was demanding the same.

साथ में बोये, साथ में काटे; साथ करें हम सारा काम।
कृषि हमारी खेत हमारा; भूमिधारी हो दोनों के नाम।

(*We sow together, we reap together; we do all the work together. The farming and farm is our, the land title should have both our names.*)

For men, the lure of a steady income from their farm while they migrated, won them over. And so, 6,800 men signed a

[6] 'Report Summaries: Swaminathan Report—National Commission for Farmers', PRS Legislative Reasearch (as viewed on 31 May 2018), http://www.prsindia.org/parliamenttrack/report-summaries/swaminathan-report-national-commission-on-farmers--662/

petition to the revenue officer in 2009, demanding ease of transfer of land titles into joint titles. This was followed by almost 7,500 women sending a similar petition two years later. In order to include the wife's name in a joint title, a registration fee of 7 per cent would have to be paid. This would be in addition to the 8 per cent that the man would have already paid for registration in his own name. This would be an added expense that families would not want or wouldn't be able to incur.

There were few instances though, like that of *cyclewali* Leelawati, where land was bought and registered in the name of the woman. To register in the name of the woman alone, the registration fee is 6 per cent. More than the low registration fee, it was the acceptance of the idea, both by men and women, that women could (and should) own land.

Anyhow, with men warming up to the idea of joint titles, there was a demand to make amends to the UPZALR (which was later repealed) and waive the registration fee. This along with other demands[7] like the provision to access credit through the spouse's KCC was made to the government through a five-point demand docket sent to the legislative assembly and the chief minister in 2012. This was followed by a *Vidhayak Samvaad Yatra* (Dialogue with the MLAs). This was

---

[7] These included: co-ownership of agricultural land, waiver of stamp duty on land transfers within the family, allowing women farmers to access facilities through their spouses KCC, 33 per cent reservation to women farmers in all government schemes and 50 per cent reservation in government and agricultural institutions.

a fairly successful exercise; nearly 25 MLAs issued a statement accepting and supporting the campaign.

Around the same time, Swaminathan tabled the Women Farmers Entitlements Bill as a private bill in the Parliament.[8] Though the Bill lapsed, it was recognition and a resounding endorsement of what the campaign had been striving to achieve. In 2015, the state government initiated to waive stamp duty in order to transfer individual titles to joint titles. A committee had been set up to assess the financial setback the state would incur if the fee were waived. The process took a backseat with elections and a subsequent change of government in Lucknow, the following year. It was eventually replaced with the Revenue Code Bill.

This also coincided with the time when the project ended. Many in the project felt that if Oxfam had continued to support and advocate, perhaps the waiver issue could have been brought to its logical end. This, of course, if the Act itself had not been repealed!

"It would have been a good time to rally around the Revenue Code Bill though," says Bhushan. The dejection, in want of a better word, is writ large on the faces of the women farmers and leaders that Aaroh Campaign nurtured.

Looking at the brighter side, it does speak volumes about what Oxfam has to offer!

---

[8] https://kractivist.files.wordpress.com/2012/06/women-farmers-bill-2012_english.pdf (as viewed on 18 June 2018).

Of Women Farmers and Women Leaders

Aaroh was a bottom-up, grassroots movement—for the women and totally owned by the women. Oxfam provided the boost and the support the project needed. It stayed behind the scenes, giving the leadership impetus and space to the women farmers who emerged as leaders and are now mentoring others.

They are the poster girls of Aaroh, in particular, and of women empowerment, in general.

Neelam, who became synonymous with Aaroh, gives full credit to Oxfam. "In the initial days, Kanchan ji laid stress on my capacity building. She had very clear ideas about gender empowerment. She was a good listener, shared information well, was very flexible and gave me full authority of the project. Though she helped establish an understanding and setting the path for the project, she never interfered in our ways of working. Oxfam nurtured grassroots leadership."

Though the campaign changed several hands—starting from Kanchan Sinha to Sabita—the ethos remained the same. It was always women farmers, first. The money wasn't much but it did wonders. The enthusiasm, dedication and drive of each and every person involved, made up for the lack of monetary resources.

The project ended in 2017, but it achieved quite a bit. It managed to turn around some of those dismal numbers. A study, on the impact of Aaroh showed: 18.7 per cent women owned land, of which, 86 per cent owned agricultural land; 29 per cent women had bought land and 65 per cent inherited it; 10 per cent women took a final call on the purchase and sale of land and in 56 per cent of the cases, it was a joint decision; 25 per cent women got the KCC and 92 per cent had access to farm loans.[9]

During a meeting with Dr Wajih in 2015, he had said that though there was no baseline to gauge the success of women[10], but government orders, notifications, acknowledgements by the MLAs and MPs, sessions in universities, awards and presence in the ATMA board were massive changes that Aaroh brought about.

Aaroh showed that women from the grassroots could be mobilised on such a large scale and that too in a state like Uttar Pradesh, where the social and gender parameters are extremely poor. The measure of its success was that men and women came together to participate in this movement for women's land rights.

Aaroh had nurtured leaders and this can be summed up in just one sentence:

महिला ही किसान है, यही देश की शान है।

(*Women are the farmers; they are the pride of the nation.*)

On last count, nearly 10,000 women were part of the Aaroh Mahila Kisaan Manch. And they have kept the momentum going.

---

[9] The study 'A Status of Women Farmers in Uttar Pradesh' was conducted by GEAG in 2014–15. This was supported by Oxfam India.

[10] This was prior to the study to assess the impact of Aaroh conducted by GEAG.

Sagara pari nila o gavira swapnara samabaya
(Samudram is a dream, which is blue and deep like a sea)

Matsyajibi narigosthira niara o ekaka parichaya
(It's a unique identity of fisherwomen groups)

Pitrutantra, prabasa, banya o batyaklista
(From the struggles of patriarchy, migration, flood and cyclone)

Narira jibana sangharsa bhitaru,
Jibika arjanara dhare alua.
(It's a ray of light for the livelihood of a woman.)

—Rukmini Panda
Gender Officer, Odisha, Oxfam India

The Power of Cooperative
Samudram
Odisha 2008–14

When Oxfam set out to support women's SHG in coastal Odisha, its main focus was to tackle the economic and social inequality that fisherwomen faced. Stories of fisherwomen not being allowed to enter a bus due to the smell, or people taking away the fish without paying for it, or being cheated by moneylenders, or being abused at home were heart-rending. Despite doing all the work, the women had no control over the money that they worked hard for.

The priority of the project was to ensure secure and sustainable livelihoods. Oxfam's Samudram project gave the women control over their resources and proved the power of the collective.

Oxfam did what the Sustainable Development Goals (SDGs) envisioned, which incidentally kicked in a year after the end of the Oxfam project. Goal 5 of SDG states that 'providing women/girls with equal access to education, healthcare, decent work and representation in political and economic decision-making processes will fuel sustainable economies and benefit societies and humanity at large'. The Samudram project showed that it was both true and possible. It gave the women rights and access to economic and natural resources, and control over their lives and livelihoods.

A subsequent outcome of the Samudram project was marine conservation. The women at Samudram live by a simple thumb-rule. "The turtle is like God to us. We believe it helps bring more fish in the sea. So we will do everything to save it from extinction." The women launched an 'artificial reef programme' to rejuvenate marine ecology and replenish fish stock. They regularly monitor the turtle population, protect them, reintroduce them in the wild and restore habitats through beach protection.

United Nations Development Programme (UNDP) started talking about 'protecting life underwater and help creating sustainable livelihoods' in their SDGs post 2015. But the women at Samudram had already begun to do their bit in order to ensure that the ecology and the welfare of their future generations are not compromised.

Samudram Maadi (Our Sea)

The Centre by the Sea

A new tap had just been installed at Samudram's procurement centre at Kothuru village in Ganjam. It had to be 'inaugurated', we were told. The tap had been functional for a couple of hours, but this was their way of welcoming us! Ranjana Das (at that time, with the Bhubaneswar office) and I were made to do the honours, never mind our reluctance. This was 2015.

In 2013, this centre had been through Phailin; it had lost its roof but quickly enough gained a new one, thanks to the women. The centre is barely 100 metres from the Bay of Bengal.

Painted white, the centre shone brightly in the August heat, sun and sand doing their trick. The centre had three rooms, a couple of toilets and a boundary wall. One room had a deep freezer and stacks of iceboxes; the stench of *Sukhua* (dried fish), spread on a makeshift platform just outside the centre, wafted through the window along with the salty breeze.

A couple of young girls, at the computer, were poring over what looked like a tally page. "Our girls take care of the accounts. We haven't been to school but they go to college," Eramma, in a red saree with a golden border, chips in proudly.

A few fisherwomen had come to meet us. Leading the pack was Buguru Chitamma. With a striking red *bindi*, about the size of a coin, and a radiant smile on her face, Chitamma stood out. A few moments into a conversation and one realises the firebrand that she is.

In fact, Nand Kishore Singh, at present with Oxfam India's Lucknow office recalls that whenever there was an issue that had to be dealt with within the community, Chitamma was the go-to person.

When Chitamma spoke, the others listened. Period.

For almost two decades, Chitamma led women of the fisherfolk community through SHGs, a fisherwomen's cooperative and finally, a producer company. The Ganjam procurement centre, one of the oldest and biggest for the producer company, is the focal trading point for the fisherwomen to collect, store, dry and export fish within and outside the state.

The producer company, Samudram, short for Samudram Trading Fisherwomen Collective Producer Company Limited, and prior to that the SHGs and cooperative, transformed the lives of the fisherwomen. Once relegated to their homes and the back end of the fishing business, they became economically independent, socially influential and savvy entrepreneurs.

They have braved the erratic seasonal changes, deep-set patriarchy, social exclusion and the unscrupulous traders to emerge unscathed and victorious. They are the women who make Samudram. They are David to Goliath!

From One Coast to Another

Chitamma, like her fellow fisherwomen, belongs to the Telugu-speaking Nolia fisherfolk community. The community, originally from Andhra Pradesh, migrated to Odisha's Ganjam district and settled in what is now the Sana Nolia Nuagaon village. This was many decades ago. Odisha, like Andhra Pradesh, has a long coastline and this for the fisherfolk community was home turf.

While there was plenty of fish (initially, at least), migration came with its share of problems. These were remote villages and they lacked basic amenities; health and education facilities were, at best, missing. To add to it, the community was grappling with social problems of alcoholism, indebtedness, gambling and child marriages. Then there were the impending natural disasters and a falling fish count, the bane of industrialisation and big trawlers.

The fisherfolk and their families, especially the smaller ones with shared boats, were caught in a debt trap. The fisherfolk took loans from local moneylenders to buy nets and boats. In order to repay their loan, they were forced to sell their catch to the same moneylenders, who doubled as fish traders, at rock bottom prices. Lack of storage space and the looming debt left the fisherfolk with no negotiating power.

The women in the community were the worst hit. Despite steering most of the work integral to the fishing business—cleaning, sorting, processing, marketing and selling, net making and repair—and taking care of all family and household needs, women were never treated as equals. They had no control over the money. Men held the purse strings and spent most of it on drinking. A few owned small patches of land. But the decision to sow or sell was never that of the woman's. There was no money left for education or health. Child marriages were rampant.

For these women, alcohol had become the curse of their lives, eating into their families and society. It had to be stopped. The women needed a way out. And Chitamma was going to be their leader; in fact, she led a revolution of sorts.

Alcohol, Debts and SHGs

In the 1990s, Chitamma led the women of her village and her neighbouring villages to raid local liquor-brewing units. They got these units shut down. Her husband did try to stop her a couple of times. "But I wasn't doing anything wrong, so there was no reason to stop," she smiles.

This was the beginning. Egged on by the success and the relentless campaigning around women empowerment and education, women of the fisherfolk community in Ganjam formed themselves into SHGs. This they did with some help from Ganjam-based NGO United Artists Association (UAA) and its CEO, Mangaraj Panda.

The SHGs shut down liquor stores then, as they continue to do today. These women are determined to stamp out alcohol and alcoholism. They continue to take turns to hold vigils and patrol the markets in order to keep tabs on drunks and brewing units. A fine of ₹500 is imposed on those caught drinking; this is divided between the informer (₹200) and the SHG (₹300).

The local police have grown to support the women; on the off chance that they don't, the women have their ways of reminding them of their duties. A few months prior to our visit in 2015, the women told us how they had *gheraoed* the police station when they refused to take action against a liquor-brewing unit. It worked.

On another occasion, the women raided a house where liquor was being brewed; they got the man arrested but it started again after a few days. The women went back again. "We told them that if they don't listen to 10 of us we would get

1,000 women. The threat worked and three shops were shut immediately," says Chitamma with her toothy grin.

After alcohol, it was the issue of indebtedness. The SHGs started with the usual saving-credit regime, which eased them out of the debt cycle to some extent. The women saved and collected anything between ₹25 to ₹100 per month; this was deposited in the revolving funds of the SHGs. The women were now able to make monthly savings. While this was empowering, this wasn't enough to get them out of the debt cycle. What they needed was institutional credit and that would have been possible if they were a cooperative.

And so Samudram, the cooperative, was born. The SHGs, with the help of UAA, federated into a cooperative in 1995. In a couple of decades, Samudram wouldn't just remain a cooperative, it would transform itself into a brand—a brand for frozen fish and dried fish, for fish pickle and prawn pickle; a brand for everything 'fish'. In fact, to keep up with the market, the women from coastal Odisha would even go online.

But, not yet.

Between 1995 and 2007, the women at Samudram dabbled with trade but they weren't able to make any breakthroughs. "The cooperative was doing business but the women were still not able to get a good price," recalls Singh, who at that time worked out of Kolkata, the Eastern India office of OGB.

They didn't have access to market linkages or storage space, the trawlers were eating into their catch, the dipping fish count spiked the production cost and the big fish traders continued to buy from them at dirt cheap rates. Trade was their Achilles heel.

But what the SHGs lacked on the business front, they more than made up for it on the social end. They were in control of their lives, they were fighting alcoholism and domestic violence and the savings enabled them to send their children to schools. In fact, the women even came together to protest against the big trawlers in 2004–05. Oxfam had supported them then, albeit briefly.

Clearly, what the cooperative did for the women was far more valuable and liberating than any money could have bought. But the best was yet to come.

Elsewhere

In 2008, OGB, through its Eastern India office, decided to support the cooperative through UAA. Having worked with the cooperative in the past—the trawler protest—OGB was convinced of the potential of the women's cooperative and their leader, Chitamma. The women just lacked the infrastructure and the information to negotiate with the traders. Oxfam was sure economic empowerment was going to turn the tide for these fisherwomen. And they could be of help.

So could Hugh Davidson. An advisor to the board of Ross Youngs, the second-largest frozen food company in the United Kingdom, Hugh felt his experience could be useful to this fisherwomen's cooperative in coastal Odisha. He also had a connection to India. Hugh's aunt had stayed in West Bengal for nearly 50 years, until 1981, and had set up three schools. She knew Mother Teresa. And he loved cricket.

Hugh also was one of the trustees of the John Davidson Trust, which felt that the Samudram project was a right fit for them. The Trust supported projects that worked towards 'providing underprivileged women and children the opportunity to reach their full potential'. Like Hugh's India connection, the Trust too was familiar with Oxfam. They were funding Oxfam's education project in Vietnam. The pieces fell in place.

And So Began Samudram's Journey

OGB and the Trust (which later became the H&S Davidson Trust) came together in a 50–50 partnership in May 2008 to support the fisherwomen's cooperative (through UAA). It would be a few months before Oxfam India, which was yet to be born, would take over. The Samudram project, as it came to be known informally, would work with nearly 3,500 fisherwomen families in four coastal districts, to double their income and help them gain financial independence.

The partnership started with a fish value chain study. "The results showed a huge gap between the coastal prices and price of fish sold in, say, Kolkata. Then there were intermediaries. These two issues had to be dealt with," says Singh. Lack of cold storage infrastructure was one of the main reasons for distressed sales, and hence the cheap rates.

The flow chart was simple. Enhancing the income would mean that the cooperative gets a fair price; in order to get a fair price, strong market linkages would have to be built; in order to have control over the market, the right infrastructure would have to be set up.

Six procurement centres in the four districts—Ganjam, Puri, Jagatsinghpur and Balasore—were set up. These centres had drying and processing areas, deep freezers, iceboxes, ice grinding machine, weighing scales, drying mats—the whole lot.

Computers were brought in and women were trained to maintain books of accounts, records of trade volume, income and expenditures. Though most of the women were illiterate, they had mastered the nitty-gritty of running the business.

"It was obvious that a lack of education or literacy does not equate in any way to lack of intelligence. These women were smart and could understand graphs and charts of prices and sales," writes Sandra Davidson in a recent email exchange. Sandra is one half of the H&S Davidson Trust.

Recalling their last visit and being understandably concerned about the sustainability of the project, Hugh insisted that Oxfam and UAA allow leaders of Samudram to make their own presentation. "We were surprised, delighted and reassured at both, the high quality of presentations and the ability to answer difficult questions," writes Hugh.

But years later, Akshaya Kumar Biswal, who took over from Nand Kishore, confesses that this suggestion by Hugh had made them a little nervous. "For the first time, community leaders were expected to present their work, challenges and their vision of Samudram. This was their visit after project shifted to the Hyderabad office," he recalls.

The meeting started and four members made the presentation led by Chitamma. "They spoke in Odiya and I translated the entire presentation to the visiting team. The presentation was so powerful and convincing that the funding support was extended for two more years."

The Unintended Consequences of SHGs

When the Davidsons' started work, the cooperative only had 70 SHGs from Ganjam with 1,529 members. More SHGs started to be formed in the districts, including Ganjam. So while the procurement centres were being set and the women trained, more women were joining the cooperative. By 2014, there were 237 SHGs from 46 villages with the strength of 3,889 women.

Talking about the project Sandra remembers, "...I became aware of the unintended consequences of the SHGs. At first, we felt the project was being delayed by the formation of these groups because we were more focused on the tangibles. But soon we realised that they were the vital factor in the success of the whole venture. The SHGs brought out the energy and the enthusiasm of the women involved and gave them the confidence they needed to succeed."

While the cooperative was taking shape and being federated at the village, district and state level, the business end was being set up. UAA brought in a trade manager, four trade supervisors, purchasing agent, two supply chain and quality executive, four SHG coordinators (to represent each district), an accountant and a manager.

In fact, during one of his visits, Hugh expressed his scepticism about engaging 14 people (15 including Mangaraj) to run the business. They held an interview with each one of them to understand their role and their achievement in the past year. A few had never faced an interview in their lives.

"They all passed the interview with flying colours. We were impressed by the clarity of their roles, their achievements and their ability to answer challenging questions. We DID need 15 people!"

The 14 ran the business like a well-oiled machine. It was simple. The trade supervisors—who were in touch with traders at the national level, regional level and local level—put up a daily price list of the different varieties of fish. These supervisors would also assess the demand in the local and regional markets. The final decision to sell a certain fish in a certain market came from this analysis.

These details would then be shared with the four SHG coordinators, who would convey the same to the federation in the districts and subsequently, the villages. Then according to the availability with the fishermen, the purchasing agent would procure from the latter. The cooperative broadened their base—they were just not procuring from within their cooperative but also outside.

Once procured, the supply chain and quality executive would then ensure that the procured fish was cleaned, graded and packed properly in iceboxes and jute bags before being transported. They went as far as Kolkata and Visakhapatnam.

Money was flowing in. Between 2007 and 2014, the average income increased by 145 per cent—from ₹12,186 to ₹29,993.

On the one hand, Samudram was gaining a foothold in the business within and outside the state, on the other, the women were giving a tough time to the local traders. In the past, the traders procured fish through auction and the fisherfolk sold their produce at any price that was offered. Lack of storage was one major reason. Storage space, thus, became the bargaining chip for the women. They had more than just one bargaining chip. They now had price intelligence.

The women refused to sell fish unless the local traders agreed to the price they quoted. This came as a shock to the traders. "They said, 'We will see how the women manage it,'" Kuntala Behera from one of the SHGs in Puri breaks into a smile recounting the first reaction of the traders. In fact, the local traders tried all kinds of tricks to break the cooperative and wean away the fishermen from Samudram.

But Samudram survived. And it flourished. The women refused to budge on the price they quoted; the local traders had to finally give in. "When the others started demanding similar prices, the local traders taunted them to go to us," says Eramma. Samudram procured from them, stored till they got a decent price and dried the rest.

Sukhua, Fish Jhuri Bhaaja and More

A business development plan, drawn with the help of an external consultancy, had mapped the market for dried fish or *Sukhua*. There was scope. But more importantly, there was a need to diversify.

State data showed 8 per cent decrease in marine catch between 2008 and 2012; this despite an overall increase in fish production by 3 per cent. Dried fish was a step towards making the cooperative sustainable. Moreover, this was a good fallback option during the months when a fishing ban would be imposed to save the Olive Ridley turtle.[1]

The women had sold *Sukhua* in the past. The difference now was that they were trained to prepare it hygienically. Plus with the backing of the cooperative, they could get a better price for the dried fish—up to almost thrice the price for their best variety. They struck a deal with the local traders and offered to supply large quantities of hygienically dried fish if the traders agreed to their price. The traders agreed. Samudram found a ready market. This was a win-win situation for the fisherfolk and the traders.

This was the first step towards a value-added product. Mangaraj had been pushing for it from the first year itself. Initially, the Davidsons had not been convinced. It came up again the next year and once again they said no. But they changed their mind soon. "The look of disappointment on his face and the importance he attached to this initiative, made us change our mind. Though the numbers didn't look very optimistic, we went for it," writes Hugh.

---

[1] PTI, 'Orissa impose marine fishing ban for 7 months', *The Hindu*, 1 November 2009, http://www.thehindu.com/news/national/other-states/Orissa-impose-marine-fishing-ban-for-7-months/article16889778.ece (as viewed on 29 March 2018).

Discussions and brainstorming sessions followed. Everyone was involved. It was during these discussions that the idea of making fish pickles, and fish and prawn *papad* came up. "An in-depth profit-loss analysis was carried out. The marketing strategy, the volume of fish that would be required—everything was worked out. There were immense possibilities," recalls Nand Kishore Singh.

Trainings in local recipes followed. Oxfam India roped in experts from Mumbai's Central Institute of Fisheries Education, and College of Fisheries from Orissa University of Agriculture and Technology (OUAT). An exposure visit to Mumbai's Indian Institute of Packaging helped them perfect their packaging, which improved sales.

The procurement centres doubled as processing centres. Later in 2014, the one at Ganjam was converted into a central processing unit, the centres at Puri and Jagatsinghpur became the hub for dry fish trade and Ganjam became the centre for value-added products. The products were taken to various exhibitions and fairs across the country and were very well received. Samudram went online and has been fairly successful at gaining some e-buyers; the fact that these products were certified by the food safety authority, helped.

Managing Director Chitamma

In 2012, the cooperative decided to go big. There was a business model, they were trained in the business of fish and its value-added products as well as the management of the business, and there was enough manpower (or rather womanpower). The next stage was to make the model sustainable.

So it was decided that Samudram the Cooperative would become Samudram the Producer Company Limited. This was a very organic decision as it came from the members of the cooperative.

"It was not an easy decision as we were not convinced about the finance management capacity within Samudram," remembers Akshaya. But instead of quelling the plan, they went ahead and strengthened the finance management system of Samudram as an institution. The software was developed which would hold all the finance-related information; training was organised for the project team and young volunteers from the community were identified to manage the finance system. Perhaps that is what the young girls at the centre were poring over!

In 2013, it was registered as Samudram Trading Fisher-women Collective Producer Company Limited. Chitamma became the managing director of the company. She continues to hold the post. Each member held shares of ₹500; this developed a capital base. The benefits of the sale were to be shared between them.

Samudram set up internal checks and balances to keep a tab on its financial health. Biannual household surveys would be held to monitor the change in income. Between 2007 and 2011, the average income increased by 124 per cent.

However, this phenomenal rise saw a dip in the following year and the year after that. This was because of reasons beyond the control of the cooperative. Restricted fishing activity, especially in Jagatsinghpur, due to the Paradip Oil Refinery, fishing bans to save the turtles and cyclone Phailin hampered the golden run. Balasore and Jagatsinghpur were the worst affected. Nevertheless, the far-sightedness of diversification kept Samudram afloat.

The fishing ban and the uncertainties of the fishing trade encouraged the women to think out of the box. On the one hand, they tried different income-generating activities in order to prevent distress migration, on the other, they went all out to protect the turtles and their nesting sites.

Samudram, as an active member of the Orissa Marine Resources Conservation Consortium, has participated in several campaigns opposing the subversion of CRZ laws and creation of SEZs. Its efforts were recognised. In 2010, Samudram received the prestigious Equator Award for 'Poverty Reduction by Conservation and Sustainable Use of Bio-Diversity'. Chitamma travelled to New York to receive the award. This is very prestigious as only 25 awards are given every two years and Samudram received one of them.

To enhance their income, the women trained in animal husbandry (duck, poultry and goat), crab fattening, rice processing, small-scale business development and cultivation of seaweed. Poultry turned out to be a huge success.

During a discussion on growing seaweeds to supplement income, Nand Kishore recalls Samudram members saying, "The way gods churned sea for finding *amrit* for a better life, we would sort out all our problems by making use of the sea."

They did experiment with seaweed but were not very successful. Win some, lose some!

What was important was that the women were eager to experiment and make the most of what was available to them. And they did. They increased their non-fisheries income by 29 per cent; they reduced their loan dependency by nearly 35 per cent.

Around the time the cooperative became a producer company, the focus of the project broadened from doubling the income to sharpening their leadership skills. The Samudram women were recognised for their business acumen. Bankers and officers of the fisheries department attended Samudram meetings whenever invited; they offered to provide credit for expanding the business. Women accessed funds from financial institutions such as National Bank for Agriculture and Rural Development (NABARD) and other government schemes and this they did collectively as Samudram as well as individuals.

Having observed Samudram from close quarters, the Integrated Coastal Zonal Management Project (ICZMP) leased 22 out of 82 solar driers to the women. With ICZMP, they were lying in a state of disuse and they believed that the women would make the best use of it. In 2017, ICZMP entered into a 10-year lease contract with Samudram to run them. This was a resounding vote of confidence for Samudram.

Life Comes a Full Circle

The men in their families, who earlier believed that SHGs were a ploy to break the family and corrupt the society, recognised and accepted them as businesswomen and social change-makers.

Men like Pitobash Behera seem to have come a long way. Back when the SHGs were coming to life, he would stop his wife, Hira, from attending meetings. There were others who beat up their wives in order to stop them.

We met Pitobash in August 2015. He insisted he never stopped Hira. The women laughed. Pitobash was Hira's proxy for the meeting as she was out on Samudram business.

At the meeting, in the sultry August afternoon, he says, "Earlier we believed women should stay at home and take care of the family. Why did they need to go out at all? We came to their meetings." He cheekily adds, "They were saving money and it would help us out of the clutches of the moneylender. It was all good."

It was, indeed, good. Women held the money. They made children's education, health and nutrition a priority. Jyoti Malick was able to send her daughter for higher studies 'thanks to Samudram'. Her husband tore their daughter's first-class matriculation certificate. "He said, 'there is no money and no need for her to continue with her studies'. But I had saved enough through Samudram. I not only got her admitted in a school but also bought her a cycle. I did not take a single penny from my husband."

Jyoti and many like her believe this would be impossible to pull off had it not been for Samudram and Chitamma. Chitamma received the Godfrey Philips Amodini Award for 'Women Empowerment' in 2011.

These women are in the thick of things—they attend gram sabha meetings, are members of School Management Committees, keep a tab on midday meals and *anganwadis*, rally against illegal land grabbing, have bank accounts and deal with officials at all levels.

During one of the visits to the *anganwadi*, Jomuna Behera found discrepancies in the distribution of Take Home Ration (THR). "We met with the block level officer to regularise its distribution. It worked." The fact that they got it done without bribing was a huge victory for the fisherwomen.

These women have come a long way. Alcoholism, domestic violence, child marriages and debt dependency have been on the wane. There are, however, the challenges of climate change that pushes the fish to deeper waters, the illegal fishing by big trawlers, pollution and decreasing fish volumes. But that's part and parcel of the business of life.

They have had profit and suffered losses, but they have done well to keep their accounts green. After all, they did replace the roof they lost to Phailin with a new one!

Samudram has had its good days and bad ones. But the women have never abandoned the spirit of *Samudram Maadi*—which, roughly translated in Telugu, means 'Our Sea'.

"I lost my daughter to pesticide. Had I paid her school fees instead, she would have been alive and working at a good place. She was an intelligent student."

—**Sadaiah Silveru**, a Dalit farmer from Akkampet in Warangal till date rues the fact that had he stopped using chemical pesticides sooner he wouldn't have had to lose his daughter. She committed suicide by drinking the same pesticide that was bought from the money that should have been her school fees.

Improved Livelihoods for Cotton Farmers, Weavers and Garment Factory Workers in South India (Also known as Cotton Textile Supply Chain project)
Andhra Pradesh and Karnataka
2002–11

Around 2002, farmer and weaver suicides saw a surge in Andhra Pradesh. Cotton farmers were on a chemical treadmill and were falling in a debt trap due to the rising input costs. On the other hand, national policies and government apathy had pulled the rug from under the weavers. Its cooperative structure was faltering. Both ends of the cotton supply chain—farmers and weavers—were in dire straits. The third component, the garment factory workers in the garment hub of Bangalore, faced all kinds of human rights violations.

The Cotton Textile Supply Chain project was an iconic project built entirely around the cotton supply chain—cotton farmers, weavers and garment factory workers. It wanted to give power to small farmers and producers so that they could demand and earn from the market a better income, improved working conditions and control of their own lives. The aim was to make trade a solution to poverty, and not part of the problem.

Oxfam Great Britain (OGB) experimented with some old, tried and tested systems like cooperatives (with some differences), a few new concepts like producer companies and a few bold steps of encouraging cotton farmers to go organic and unionising women workers. This was still 2002! The conventional trade unions were not prepared to take up women's issues who were suffering mental, physical and sexual harassment at the workplace.

The project was complex. It ranged from dealing with big international apparel companies like GAP (as part of putting pressure on local manufacturers for compliance with labour laws) to the pesticide manufacturers and dealers in the villages (who opposed the fact that farmers were moving from chemicals and going organic).

The nine-year project met with mixed success but it proved to be an invaluable learning ground. Those associated with the project at different stages call it a 'lab of sorts'. The project, after all, did give the blueprint for several international campaigns later. The project was ahead of its times—whether it was going organic or forming a trading company or fighting for basic human rights.

The project gave: a farmer trader company (which wasn't as successful)—Oorvi; a brand the weavers built and outlasted the life of the project—Kargha; and a women's labour union that has become a voice to reckon with in the garment hub of Bangalore—Garment Labour Union (GLU).

The project laid the foundation for the Private Sector Engagement work that is being implemented by OIN at the moment. Oxfam is working on Business and Human Rights Framework now, but this kind of advocacy was done almost 10 years ago when the project worked with the garment factory workers. Those involved with the project, at different stages, also worked closely with the Ministry of Corporate Affairs to draw the CSR Voluntary Guidelines.

So all's well that ends well.

For a Decent Living

The 22-Day Trip

Nishant Pandey went with an unusual request to his boss. He wanted the official car, driver and a no-questions-asked travel approval. This was in 2002. "Those were the days of maintaining travel logs. But I didn't really have a travel plan. I just wanted to explore a few things," says Nishant in a phone conversation in July 2018. He is now based in the United States. He did get the permission. He was out for 22 days, travelling the length and breadth of undivided Andhra Pradesh.

Nishant, a banker in Jammu and Kashmir, was hired by OGB to lead a new livelihood project in South India. But there was no blueprint. All Nishant knew was that the new project had to make good on two essential themes—one, ensuring farmers learn to harness the power of the markets and earn better returns for their produce, and two, leveraging trade as a way to reduce poverty.

He started his travel from Warangal, triggered by the innumerable stories of farmer suicides in the local newspapers. Traditionally, the cotton farmers supplied cotton to the weavers. Now if this was a producer (farmer)–buyer (weaver) relationship as they were part of the same supply chain, one was likely to exploit or dominate the other and it could still make some sense if one of the two were suffering losses and hence, forced to commit suicide.

"But in this case, neither got a good deal. So there had to be something inherently wrong in both what the farmers and weavers were doing and the situations that they were in. And clearly, someone else in the middle was making all the money."

This is what he wanted to explore. How was it possible that no one in the market was better off? This peculiar situation of the market became clearer during his almost a month-long journey across the state.

As it turned out, indeed, someone did benefit while the two ends of the supply chain—farmers and weavers—struggled to survive. This someone was the ginning and spinning mills. And this understanding was at the heart of OGB's Cotton Textile Supply Chain (CTSC) project.

A Jigsaw Puzzle

The ginning and spinning mills were a marker of India's colonial legacy. When the American Civil War broke out in the United States in 1861, Britain found it hard to source the long-staple cotton that its domestic industries needed. So, India's colonial masters disrupted the traditional Indian markets—where farmers sold short-staple cotton to weavers directly—by introducing the mills. The trouble was, as was evident in Andhra Pradesh, over time it was the mills that were making all the profits; they paid paltry sums to the farmers while selling processed cotton to the weavers at exorbitant rates.

Neither the farmers nor the weavers had enough cushion to prosper. A straightforward solution would have been for the farmers to use the mills to process the cotton and then sell that to the weavers directly. But, of course, that would require collectivisation. Individual farmers did not have the bargaining power to deal with the mills or indeed, hire them. The margins were huge. If the cotton farmers sold their cotton to the mills at ₹100, the mills would gin, spin and price it at ₹210 for weavers, while the actual cost incurred would be around ₹30.

Low remuneration for their produce was just one part of the problem for the farmers. Over time, their input costs had gone up considerably. A key cost centre was the price of chemical pesticides, which accounted for almost 40–50 per cent of the total production cost. This not only made production more costly, but also meant that a crop failure could increasingly spell doom for a farmer and his family.

The use of chemical pesticides also had a debilitating impact on the health of the farmers. In Warangal in 2001, there were 12 deaths and over 40 persons were affected by the exposure to pesticides while spraying. Then there were the daily niggles of skin and eye irritation, nausea, stomach ailments and dizziness. Here, the need was felt to get the farmers off the pesticides treadmill and get them to go organic.

Like farmers, weavers who were already struggling because of their dealings with the mills (they purchased the same cotton at a much higher price) had other problems. In particular, the National Textile Policy of 1985, which liberalised the textile industry and opened it up to greater privatisation, ended up being highly disadvantageous for over 40 lakh traditional weavers. That's because the policy was biased towards the 'commercially viable power looms'. Unlike states such as Maharashtra and Gujarat that modernised and integrated the new production process or Tamil Nadu that adapted to the changing market, Andhra Pradesh struggled. That's because it neither had the monetary resources to go modern nor the market-savvy master weavers to adapt to changing consumer tastes.

The 1990s dealt the final blow to the Andhra weavers when the Andhra Pradesh State Handloom Cooperative Society (APCO)—set up in the 1970s to help handloom weavers (and their cooperatives) with finance and marketing facilities—became defunct by 1998. This led to the loss of market share, piling up of stocks, lack of jobs, mounting debts, starvation, hunger deaths and suicides. The solution, here, was to regroup the weavers to enhance their bargaining power to buy yarn and sell clothes, upgrading their skills to meet the market demands and advocating for weaver-friendly policies. The ideal situation would be to link cotton farmer cooperatives with weaver cooperatives. OGB did take a shot at it but wasn't very successful. The project was way ahead of its time or monetary capacity.

Nishant's visit to the mills took him to Bangalore, also to the third part of the supply chain, the garment industry hub. The industry was rife with sexual, physical and economic exploitation of its women workers. But the lack of awareness, avenues or agency of these women who were migrants from some of the most marginalised communities, let manufacturers stomp all over their labour and human rights. Here again, the solution was to collectivise women workers into unions and train them on labour laws and human rights so that they could fight for their rights. The other part was to advocate with international brands, which sourced their garments from these units, to provide fair wages and decent living; this would fit very well with Oxfam's Make Trade Fair Campaign.

Joining the Dots

By the end of his trip, Nishant had a blueprint; it was now about getting the right people on board. He draws an analogy with making a film. "You can do it two ways. One, select the actors and then write the script. Two, write a script and then select the actors best suited for the film. OGB chose the second option." There were organisations working with farmers, weavers and garment factory workers but they were operating in silos. Oxfam was going to bring them together and look at it from a supply chain perspective.

For farmers, Oxfam partnered with four NGOs in Warangal district. The four complemented each other and fit the bill of collectivising and going chemical-free. Jangaon-based Centre for Rural Operations Programmes Society (CROPS) had the technical expertise of non-pesticide management/ organic farming. Warangal-based Modern Architects for Rural India (MARI) was good at collectivising farmers. Also from Warangal were Sarvodaya Youth Organisation (SYO) and Pragathi Seva Samithi (PSS) who worked closely with Dalit farmers and women SHGs respectively.

For the garment factory workers, Civil Initiatives for Development and Peace-India (CIVIDEP), a Bangalore-based organisation was brought on board. They were already working on the impact of globalisation on employment and labour rights and felt the need to build a broad coalition of workers; Oxfam was looking to empower women in the supply chain. The two worked well together. Munnade and GLU, the right mix of social and political organisations, emerged from the project; this gave a lot of heft to women's voice. This work on labour and human rights laid the foundation for Oxfam India's Private Sector Engagement (PSE) work on tracking and ranking industries based on the UN's guiding principle of Business and Human Rights.

To work with weavers, Oxfam needed to collaborate with a partner that would collectivise weavers to come out of the shadows of unscrupulous moneylenders and exploitative master weavers, build institutional linkages and bring them up to speed with the dynamic market. There were enterprising individuals but lacked organisational backing to take up the scale of work that Oxfam was proposing.

There was a union of weavers at Chirala that Oxfam contemplated supporting but again they were not eligible for foreign funds and neither was another NGO, Sanghamitra, that was actually working very closely with weavers in Nalgonda. Finally, Oxfam went with Hyderabad-based Chetana Society led by environmental activist, Dr Narasimha Reddy Donthi, who, among other things, was working on the development of the handloom sector. Centre for Handloom Information and Policy Advocacy (CHIP) in Chirala, an outcome of this project, worked with weavers and deep-dived into policy advocacy.

This was perhaps the trickiest bit. The weavers' component needed to open itself to the market but with an activist at the helm, there was a constant tug of war of principles. This was expected in a project that was way ahead of its time and was still trying to strike the correct notes. Though things happened in fits and starts, it had its sunny moments. The weavers set up a handloom trading company (HTC) and built Kargha, a handloom brand that outlasted the life of the project.

The canvas of the project was large. This meant that some strands worked better than others, and some lasted longer than others. The project was about harnessing the power of people, changing ways of working, bringing them out on the streets, even, to make them heard. But all of this took some convincing, a lot of time and a lot of hard work by each and everyone involved.

School Fee or a Bottle of Pesticide

It was 2003, a regular year for Suguna and Sadaiah Silveru, Dalit farmers of Akkampet village. They grew some cotton and some vegetables to get by on their small patch of land. They had three children—two girls and a boy. Their teenage daughter, Shravanthi, the eldest of the lot and a good student, needed money for her school fees. This was around the same time that Sadaiah needed to buy pesticides for his cotton crop. The money was limited. They weighed their options—school fee or a bottle of pesticide. They eventually decided in favour of the latter; a decision they were going to regret for the rest of their lives. Without fees, Shravanthi had to drop out of school. Furious, one day in 2004, she ended her life—drank the same pesticide that was bought with the money that was meant to be her school fees.

Shravanthi's suicide jolted them out of their resistance to organic farming. SYO had started working in this village in Atmakur mandal in Warangal's rural district in 2002 as part of a pilot that Oxfam ran for the CTSC project. The Silverus' were not keen on giving up conventional farming. "We weren't sure initially. But our daughter's death made us realise the hazard of overspending on chemical farming as well as keeping such dangerous chemicals at home," said Sadaiah when we met him in 2017.

There were others like seventy-year-old Panduga Mughalaya, one of the well-off farmers belonging to the Backward Caste (BC). Though his father was a natural farmer, he started using chemicals because the 'government started giving it for free' (he was probably referring to the years around the Green Revolution). He opted for natural farming after he started realising the health impact these chemicals had on him. This was in 2003, the year Oxfam's project started in full swing.

Farmers had to be persuaded to go organic if they had to come out of the debt cycle, reduce their expenses on chemical inputs and improve their health. This would upset the apple cart. Further, since Oxfam was pushing for organic, all contiguous fields had to be chemical-free; it was thus important to get a buy-in from the farmers. It began with encouraging farmers to convert small patches of their land into chemical-free plots. They were taught to replace chemical pesticides with concoctions of cow dung and urine, milk, curd, chillies, garlic and neem. Oxfam along with the partner NGOs set up vermicomposting pits so farmers could prepare their own fertiliser. In 2017, some farmers were still using those pits.

The next step was weaning farmers off from their over-dependence on monocropping and encouraging multi-cropping. Most farmers were marginal monocroppers and cotton farmers; they were motivated to go for pulses and vegetables. This would reduce their dependence on markets for their nutritional needs as well as improve the soil health. In addition, the project provided some money for poultry and buffalo; they could directly use their dung as farm manure and milk as additional income.

Unlike the Silverus', there were some like Tukya of Rollakal village in the Parvathagiri mandal, who were already converts—both to monocropping and non-pesticide management farming. His five-acre field stands close to the road that leads into his village.

When we visited him in December 2017, a large part of his land had recently been cleared and was being mulched. This was the cotton patch that he was planning to replace with maize in the next season. Tukya stood on a bund, at the junction of his banana and turmeric plots, packing baby brinjals into gunny bags for the market. The vegetable patch was tucked away behind the turmeric field.

"This is all organic. You can take a walk inside. You will feel the difference." Despite a packed day ahead, Tukya walked us through the banana grove and the nitty-gritty of going organic. He came to his favourite anecdote, I am told. Back in 1997, he had spotted some pests and was examining his crop, when an inquisitive passer-by stopped and enquired. The passer-by explained the pest cycle to him—eggs, larva and the works. This piqued Tukya's interest. He kept in touch with the passer-by and learnt about the growth cycle of pests, the impact of pheromone traps, light traps and bird perches, and preparing chemical-free pesticides. He had become a convert.

The passer-by was Dr MA Qayum of the Centre for World Solidarity (CWS), one of the pioneers of Non-Pesticide Management (NPM) in the state.

By the time Oxfam started its project in 2003, Tukya was already an expert and a useful resource person. To this day, Tukya and his farm remain exemplary. Also exemplary is the Enabavi village, also in Warangal. A big board at the entrance of the village announces an 'organic and GM-free village'. By 2003, when Oxfam joined hands with CROPS, Enabavi had gone chemical-free. Enabavi's reputation helped get the buy-in from other farmers in neighbouring and far off villages. Though it was labour-intensive, the money that the farmers saved on the input cost, as well as the health impacts, was a good enough pull factor.

Then came the turn of forming farmer cooperatives or Mutually Aided Cooperative Societies (MACS); this would bring all cotton farmers to the negotiating table and with strong bargaining powers. Each partner NGO had to form one MACS. Silveru, Tukya, Panduga all became members of these cooperatives; they also served as board members of their MACS. These would enable cotton farmers to source non-BT seeds, prepare natural pesticides and vermicompost, share technical know-how, negotiate for a better price for organic cotton and establish international market linkages for its ginned and spun cotton.

The Oxfam Building

While trying to line up a field trip to Warangal, I contacted a MARI old hand—a stern-sounding Ramamurthy. Trying to talk to him through a bad network, the only thing I could understand in our very first conversation was that I should reach a particular spot in Warangal by 7 AM (from Hyderabad it would mean leaving at about 4:30 AM) and that there was an Oxfam building that I should visit. It was a tad difficult for me to imagine what an Oxfam building was doing in a Warangal village or why this building was so important for me to visit.

I reached on time the next day, met Ramamurthy, had mini-tiffin for breakfast and headed to the village where we met Tukya and the others. Then we went to the 'Oxfam Building'. This was actually a large storehouse on the side of the road, with trees along the boundary wall (some of which planted by the Oxfam team during one of the visits in the past), a wide gate for trucks to roll in and out of and a large shed that was the open office for the storehouse. This building was part-funded by Oxfam to serve as a store for pre-ginned organic cotton while the best prices were being negotiated for.

The Navjeevan Organic Farmers MACS of Parvathagiri mandal, to which the 'Oxfam Building' belongs, has been one of the most successful models. Over the years, the building has been repaired and reinforced by different agencies, the cooperative itself and even the local MLA. They started with cotton procurement as was planned in the project; they expanded to paddy procurement in 2014, which has now become a roaring business.

With cotton, as was the plan, they sold it directly to the ginners and they were paid directly and almost immediately through the society. With a society to back them up, they had bargaining power and could choose the best-paying ginner. When the farmers were selling their cotton to Cotton Corporation of India (CCI), they had to pay extra charges for handling, labour and storing. Moreover, since they were organic farmers they were able to sell it at a premium. Paddy collection has thrived. In fact, they had to acquire some more land—as an extension to this storehouse—to store the paddy. By 2016, nearly 700 farmers were selling their paddy through this cooperative society.

The cooperative societies were based on membership fees; services and credit were going to be provided through this. And this was entirely voluntary. Women's participation was made mandatory. That women did a large chunk of the farm-based work—especially the labour-intensive weeding, spraying, cotton picking—and yet had no control over money or farm-related decisions was recognised and the project set out to correct this anomaly. Since women SHGs were already a strong institution in the state, the CTSC project worked closely with these women.

Aruna and Sujatha of Navjeevan recall Murali, from MARI, going to the villages to talk about gender equality, the role of women in agriculture and why they should join the cooperative society. "He made us realise that we were equal partners in farming. He ensured that we became members of the cooperative society," they said as we walked out of Tukya's field before heading to 'the Oxfam Building'. In fact, women played a crucial role in pushing their husbands to go organic. Oxfam's emphasis on women participation and the commitment was reiterated by the fact that a gender officer was assigned exclusively for this project.

In 2017, Ramamurthy was working with the MACS members to make the society sustainable and more profitable.

Back then the society was contemplating a few questions such as the number of employees they should hire with decent wages so that they could service the far off villages, how can they sustain an annual income of ₹25 lakh and if they should set up cotton ginning and rice mills.

Though it has been nearly eight years since the project ended, a few good things continue till date: CROPS continues to work on NPM and organic farming; MARI has a model cooperative system; PSS evolved its MACS into a farmer producer organisation which apart from cotton and paddy procurement has diversified into dairy and fisheries and credit to farmers; and, SYO has continued its focus on Dalit farmers.

Weaving a Better Future

Lakshman joins us for lunch at the Bhoodan Pochampally rural tourism complex, about 50 km from Hyderabad and the hub of Pochampally silk. He was taking a break from the end of season Kargha sale at the complex. On sale were sarees, stoles, furnishing and running material in fabulous ikat print to choose from. The weft and double ikat pattern, unique to handloom and not replicable on the power loom, sets the Kargha brand aside. It was an intelligent move by the Oxfam project.

In the mid-1990s, as power looms took over, a lot of its fabric started being sold as handloom, further eating into the handloom sector. At the time when the cotton project started, the weavers were badly cornered by government policies. "The weavers had such deep-rooted problems which a 10-year project was unlikely to solve. But a start had to be made somewhere," says Sudha Rani Mullapudi. Sudha was on the project between 2005 and 2009 and worked very closely with farmers and weavers. After she left Oxfam, she joined Chenetha Colour Weaves, the handloom trading company that Oxfam was supporting. And now she runs her own social enterprise and continues to work closely with the weavers.

"So the weavers were formed into MACS, just like the farmers," she says. But then weaver had already been in cooperatives, in the past, which had collapsed. "This was different. These gave the power to the weavers to deal with private players and markets, instead of being dependent on government," Sudha explains. This was different because they were self-reliant, competitive and entirely owned by the members. They were better because they included women, focused on institution building, pulled the weavers out from the clutches of an exploitative master weaver and focused on skill development. Earlier the weavers were only skilled for APCO's requirement and the Janta Cloth Scheme. Through these MACS, the weavers were trained on new methods of dyeing and design to meet the demands of the market. Training was given to 486 weaver families in the Nalgonda district.

An handloom trading company of MACS was formed under the name Chenetha Colour Weaves (CCW) Pvt Ltd, which took the responsibility of marketing the handloom product of the weavers. They were paid a premium. This encouraged the other weavers working under other master weavers, who exploited and underpaid artisans, to demand equal remuneration.

The handloom product was sold under the brand Kargha. And Lakshman, who we met, was in charge of marketing. The owner of a single loom almost a decade ago, he now supports

10 weavers. Technically he is a master weaver but prefers to call himself a 'small entrepreneur'. Also in the room were a weaver couple, Latha and Venkatasam. In the past, Latha had been on the board of CCW. She also won an award for graphic ikat designing, something that is considered a male forte. Both continue to work for master weavers but on their own terms and conditions.

In the entire project, that was very aspirational and way ahead of its times, perhaps the weavers got the short end of the stick. From Oxfam's point of view, there wasn't enough money in the project. "There were no producer companies, no CSR Act or Section 25 (where companies could implement their CSR through Section 8 companies floated by them). Had there been any of this, the handloom trading company could have had some big capacity investors and the weavers model would have been successful," says Sudha. In fact, Sudha's passion for the weavers' cause and the project even after all these years is very infectious.

From Oxfam's partners' points of view, too, the funds weren't enough. "The weavers should have been supported financially for at least six cycles; instead they were supported for just two cycles (only 90 days). It would have made the weavers a little more sustainable," remarks T Yadagiri. He was from Sanghamitra, an NGO that worked closely with weavers, but was without an FCRA (Foreign Contribution (Regulation) Act, 2010) registration, which meant they could not take funds from OGB. They started working through Chetana Society but the alliance didn't last long.

The project was able to pull weavers out of exploitative markets and master weavers, failing cooperatives and lack of market access and knowledge. These it did to a large extent. It also wanted to tackle this issue of the high cost of yarn, which it was hoping to do by linking the farmer trading company with the handloom trading company but that was something it wasn't able to achieve.

But this was an experiment, which had some excellent takeaways. Women, for one, were the biggest gainers. They were encouraged to venture into graphic designing and to sit on the looms, both considered male forte; they also became board members of CCW. Designers were brought on board, which helped weavers explore new avenues. Since CCW increased the salary every year, the bargaining skills improved and some amount of reverse migration took place; this was particularly important since weavers' salaries had stagnated for nearly a decade prior to 2002.

Since the weaver's strand of work had Dr Narasimha Reddy Donthi at the helm of affairs, its advocacy with the government was very strong. The efforts paid off, albeit briefly, when the government decreased the import duty on raw material from 25 per cent to 5 per cent; the high price of silk yarns was one of the main reasons for the crisis in the handloom sector.

The other big win was the loan waiver of ₹312 crore to weavers. This would have just remained a mere announcement had CHIP not pushed it with State Human Rights Commission and gone all guns blazing to the media and policymakers; in August 2010, ₹109 crore was released which is estimated to have benefitted about 1,200 cooperatives and 50,000 families.

Oorvi: A Plan Ahead of Its Time

Like the handloom trading company, there was a farmer trading company, Oorvi. At some point, the idea was to link the two so that the weavers could source the ginned and spun cotton directly from the organic farmers. Since the project wanted to use the market to pull people out of poverty and ensure that the cooperatives lasted longer than the project, a market-based solution in the form of a farmer trading company was introduced.

Back in 2002, the concept of growing organic itself was daring enough and to convince a large number of farmers to go organic at once was even more daring. Substantial effort was put in the form of exposure visits and ensuring a steady stock of supplies of natural fertilisers and pesticides. If a cooperative was formed, they could procure cotton in bulk and that would mean better bargaining power. Bulk would also ensure that cotton could be stored until they got a better price for their cotton, hire the best-paying ginner and build linkages to national and international market on their own.

But trade links could not be built. The glitch was insufficient working capital. "Oxfam couldn't have gone for the debt-equity structure (Oxfam 51 per cent–Company 49 per cent) because that would mean exposing themselves to the market. This was a big decision and it went to the board of trustees. Oxfam wasn't ready for this. Then Oxfam wasn't in a position to give grants to the company directly. So though it routed the grants through MACS, the money wasn't enough," explains Amit Vatsyayan, who managed the Oxfam project between 2005 and 2008. Amit was brought on board given his past experience of working with Pochampally weavers in Nalgonda.

He goes on to elaborate, "While the concept of Oorvi was fantastic, it soon became a monetary and logistical nightmare. It had to store all that cotton till they got a good price and also ensure immediate payment to farmers while the stock remained unsold." Both the capital and operational expenditure needed to be covered and Oorvi didn't have that kind of money.

"There was no concept of impact investment at that time around 2005. It was around the same time that the 24 Letter Mantra chain began and it thrived because it had money to fund it throughout. Rules for foreign investments in agriculture have changed since. If the project were to be carried out now, Oxfam would be better placed to execute it," Amit explains.

Though the weavers' cooperative and trading company would have been a bigger success in the present circumstances, the work with the garment factory workers in neighbouring Karnataka was spot on.

Women Power

We had taken permission to be a fly on the wall at a GLU meeting. So on a Sunday afternoon, in December 2017, we pulled up on the side of a busy crossroad in Peenya. One of the industrial hubs, Peenya is on the Bangalore-Tumkur highway. This is where many garment manufacturing units are; earlier they were concentrated on the Mysore Road. But in the last few years, they began to move to Peenya.

The meeting was at GLU's office—on the first floor of a corner building. The pile of slippers at the entrance was a clear giveaway of a full house. There were nearly 80 women in attendance; garment factory workers, seated on chairs lined in neat rows. In front of the room were police officers (men and women). The meeting was organised to apprise the local police about cases of sexual exploitation and physical harassment in garment factories.

The point of this Munnade meeting was to tell the police 'the next time we come to the police station, listen to us'. The police gave a patient hearing and promised to take action. The credit for this goes to GLU—the origins of which lie in the CTSC project. Sexual exploitation in garment manufacturing units is as rampant at this point as it was back in 2002 when the project started. The difference now was that women workers had the backing of GLU to take up these issues head-on.

As part of CIVIDEP's ongoing work with the women in garment manufacturing units, they conducted a survey of cases registered in the labour court. Two points were loud and clear—one, garment manufacturing is a formal industry governed by labour laws; two, though violations around labour rights, harassment of workers (sexual and physical), unfair dismissals and withholding employee benefits were well-known yet there were almost no cases in the labour courts. "There were instances but no cases," says Gopinath K Parakuni, general secretary, CIVIDEP-India.

More horror stories came out at meetings that CIVIDEP and Oxfam had with the women workers. Yashoda recalls, "The supervisor often spoke at length of 'bras and zip in men trousers'. Those who played along were promoted, those who didn't, remained on the shop floor, or worse, were forced to leave." Physical harassment was rife—if any worker was slow, the supervisors would pull their ears or hit them. The conditions were inhuman, forcing women to leave. There were no crèches; to avoid maternity benefits and leaves, pregnant workers would be dismissed on some pretext or the other; there was no canteen; toilet breaks were discouraged; the working conditions were unhygienic.

The fact that these women migrated and belonged to the lowest socio-economic strata made them even more vulnerable. They were neither aware of the laws nor did they have the resources to see these cases through prolonged court hearings. They had no support system. The conventional trade unions were supportive but women's issues weren't their priority. They were sceptical because they felt it was challenging to mobilise and organise them and develop them as leaders.

Moreover, women workers were hesitant to join trade unions lest they lost their job due to sheer association. Some thinking out of the box needed to be done; unionisation could not begin with the classical confrontationist approach. CIVIDEP formed Munnade, sort of a pre-trade union social organisation. The Munnade drove home two points: one, that women could access their rights only if they were organised under the law; two, that there were several provisions under the law that safeguarded trade unions.

Yashoda first came across CIVIDEP at a meeting in a worker's house in 2002. She persuaded a few others to join her. Her enthusiasm and her interest in labour rights brought her into the Oxfam project fold. That was the last year she worked in any garment factory. Yashoda became a key activist.

She was there at gate meetings at the end of the shift and in their colonies on holidays to encourage women to join.

"Women workers are a floating population. Since the turnover of labourers was very high in Bangalore, we focused on forming solidarity groups in localities instead of forming working groups in the factories. It was easier to reach out to them in their homes where they were more settled, more accessible and less vulnerable," says Gopinath.

As more and more women joined Munnade, they realised that certain cases couldn't be solved by the organisation since they were not registered as a union. In 2006, CIVIDEP supported the formation of Garment and Textile Workers Union (GATWU) and Mahila Garments Karmikara Munnade. The former was a trade union, first of its kind in the garment manufacturing sector, that took the mantle of filing cases with the labour commissioner regarding violation of labour rights of garment factory workers, provident fund, etc. The latter was a collective of garment workers to meet the social needs of garment workers.

However, in 2011, a few women leaders walked out of GATWU, alleging sexual harassment by the male members, and formed an all-women trade union, the GLU. This was registered a year later. They also left the Karmikara Munnade and started Munnade Social Organisation (MSO) as an NGO the same year. Yashoda was one of the many who walked out of GATWU and formed GLU.

While MSO takes up cases of domestic violence and sexual harassment, and provides community crèche and tuition support to children, GLU takes up issues of sexual violence at the workplace, unfair working conditions and delayed disbursal of salaries and benefits. It has a membership of 3,000 members.

"It has given us awareness and the strength to fight for our rights. GLU and Munnade have helped bring about changes in the lives of the lot of us," says Saroja. Like Yashoda, she too stopped working in a garment factory after getting associated with CIVIDEP. The long years of association has given the women the agency to question and to stand up for what is rightfully theirs.

And the importance of GLU and MSO in their lives is clear from the fact that when Oxfam's project ended in 2011, they worked without salary and sold some of their jewellery to keep the office and staff of MSO and GLU going for almost a year before the next funding support came in.

It hasn't been easy for the women associated with the union—they have been threatened and harassed—but they know that they have the backing of 3,000 members and this is a huge boost to their morale. Women workers, member or not, prefer to come to GLU to solve their cases rather than rely on some 'biased' committee within the factory or to the police.

As the meeting at Peenya came to a close, members started queuing up for lunch. There were a few first-timers who had come to air their grievances before the police. Before they could head for the meals, they huddled around Yashoda and Saroja with questions about the union and how they could join. The duo patiently responded to each one of them. The union seemed to be their only hope for providing a decent living.

"*We should get more children back to school.*"

—**Alfiyah,** Class Six, Chak Ahmedpur Poorva Madhyamik Vidyalaya, Raebareli municipality. She is a member of the Bal Sansad and she, along with her other classmates, checks on students who skip school for more than a couple of days. She talks to parents and convinces them to send their children to school. If that doesn't work, she gets teachers to intervene. It has worked. The school achieved 100 per cent retention.

Education for All
Lokmitra. Samarth Foundation. Sikshasandhan
Uttar Pradesh and Odisha (ongoing)

Here are a few facts and numbers to mull over:

- There is a declining trend in the number of enrolments at both the primary and upper primary level.
- The dropout rates remain high with 6.35 per cent children dropping out at the primary level[1]
- Dropout is the highest among the Scheduled Tribes at a near 9 per cent.
- Data on out-of-school children, if available, are at best unreliable.

Uttar Pradesh's education department came up with a benign figure of 27,695 out-of-school children (2018–19). State Collective of Right to Education (SCoRE), the state arm of the Right To Education (RTE) Forum, conducted a sample survey in 26 gram panchayats and found 1,501 out-of-school children. A detailed analysis puts this number to approximately 34 lakh out-of-school children; of which about 39 per cent are Dalit and 22 per cent are Muslim.

It is clear that many children are not making it to school. Whichever lens you look at out-of-school children from, the bottom line is that they are deprived of the opportunity for education, of a better future and of making the society more equal. Children drop out for a variety of reasons. There are infrastructure and logistical issues—not enough classrooms, no proper toilets, no boundary walls, no water facility, delay in distribution of books and uniform. Then there are either too few teachers or none at all. Those who do go to school

---

[1] http://www.careindia.org/wp-content/uploads/2018/12/Status%20report18.pdf

are deployed in non-academic work in gross violation of RTE Act.[2] Then there is the medium of education.

Deep-set patriarchal social norms push girls to get married and raise a family. Many girls are pulled out of school or not sent to one to help out in household chores or take care of the siblings while the parents migrate. Boys aren't better off either. They are seen as future breadwinners and are expected to help with farming and tending cattle from a very young age.

Oxfam's work around education has been varied. From making parents (School Management Committees) responsible of their duties and rights towards their child's education to forming Bal Sansads (children's collectives) which give children the power to demand their rights from the school; from supporting *Bhasha Sikshaks*, who teach in the mother tongue of the Adivasi children, to retaining the interest of children in studies through sports, it has smashed some very deep-set patriarchal social norms in the society.

There is, however, a common thread that runs through its work, that is, to get children from some of the most marginalised communities back to school so that they get the opportunity to decent education and a shot at smashing inequality.

---

[2] Engagement of teachers in the census, election duty and disaster response (three kinds of duties) are allowed under RTE. But, the deployment of teachers in non-academic work by education departments or district administrations is a gross violation of the RTE Act.

Kuwar Gets Back to School

Parents, Leaders

"छः साल हो गये होंगे अध्यक्षा के पद पर। नहीं। संजय जी?"
("*It has been six years on the president's post. No? Sanjay ji?*")

Sharda looks quizzically at Sanjay. I look quizzically at Sanjay. Sanjay is a project coordinator with Lokmitra. Sanjay and I were meeting Sharda, a very active and vocal School Management Committee (SMC) member. Rather, the president as it turns out.

The confusion around the number of years stems from the fact that the 15-member SMC, 11 of which are parents, are elected every two years. But she is quick to clear the air. "लोग कहते हैं 'तुम सब जगह जाती हो', तुम सबसे बात कर सकती हो', 'तुम बने रहो'।" ("*People say, 'you go everywhere', 'you can talk to everyone', 'You should remain the president'.*") And so here she is.

We were catching up with Sharda at her home at Kallu Ka Purwa in Raebareli's municipality area. She lives in a one-room house, with her husband and four children. The husband, who worked part-time as a painter and part-time at a brush-manufacturing unit, was away. Her children were at school. We sat chatting on a bench just outside her home, under the shade of a large banyan tree which was a brilliant idea on a hot and humid August afternoon.

In the course of our conversation, she points towards the boundary wall of the Kallu Ka Purwa primary school. The school—the one she is the SMC president of—is a stone's throw away. Unlike most SMC members or even presidents, Sharda drops by the school at least once every day. And on some days, three times. That is how she manages to keep a tab on the midday meals and the attendance of children. And like most SMC members, she started off being enlisted as a member yet completely oblivious to either the existence of SMC or their role in the committee.

It was only after a chance meeting with Lokmitra—when she was trying to get her eldest daughter readmitted to school—that she came to know of the committee and the part she could play. The sparks of her leadership skills were evident even back then—once she understood the admission process, she brought back three girls in her neighbourhood who had dropped out of school in the last one year. This was around 2011. The SMCs, where they work, have played a crucial role in getting out-of-school children back to schools and ensuring 100 per cent retention.

Emboldened and excited about the role parents can play in their children's education, she went all out attending SMC and federation meetings and statewide consultations; she participated in rallies and sit-ins at Lucknow. Not only has she become the go-to person in Kallu Ka Purwa and the neighbouring areas for all things related to schools, she has also become a poster girl of sorts for SMCs. And this is how it happened.

After the RTE Act was rolled out on 1 April 2010, there was a lot of advocacy around the proper implementation of the Act, appointment of teachers, the formation of SMC's and so on and so forth. In Uttar Pradesh, this was done through SCoRE and BSM or Basic Siksha Manch. SCoRE, formed in 2009, was a network of NGOs, CSOs, academia, journalists,

SMC collectives, educationists and education activists across the state; they spearheaded the advocacy in the capital. The Manch, on the other hand, was the brainchild of Lokmitra and followed a similar structure; it ensured that that 50 per cent of its members were parents—parents who were SMC members. Parents like Sharda.

So as it happened in 2013, SCoRE and BSM held several meetings with the Sarva Siksha Abhiyaan appointed director, Sheetal Verma, and the State Commission for Protection of Child Rights (SCPCR) newly appointed chair, Juhi Singh.

"A few of us went to meet them with our demands for the timely elections of SMCs, of women in leadership roles in these committees and a ruling to mandate women as either president or vice president of the SMC. They asked a simple thing, 'You are doing all this advocacy for parents and women, but where are they?'" recalls Binod Sinha. He is the programme coordinator with Oxfam's Lucknow office.

The next thing he knows, a group of parents from different SMCs are brought to Lucknow. Sharda was supposed to present the case for women participation. "I admit I wasn't very confident," smiles Binod after all these years. "And I was so wrong. When she started, everyone in the room realised that she was actually the best person who could have put the case for women in SMCs and the role they can play in improving the situation of the government schools."

Five years on, Sharda still recalls the day when she spoke on behalf of the parents in the meeting but she can't understand what the fuss was all about. She had just spoken her heart out—like she continues to do even now. But what all that advocacy did—and she is inadvertently a part of it—was that the state passed a government order in August 2013 making it compulsory for all SMCs in the state to have at least one woman as either the president or the vice president.

So with the reputation of—"तुम सब जगह जाती हो", "तुम सबसे बात कर सकती हो" (*"you go everywhere"*, *"you can talk to everyone"*—she continues to lead her SMC. And Sharda isn't the only one.

Nearly 50 parents were present for a block SMC meeting in the lawns of the Rahi block development office. There was equal participation from men and women; a few women were there with their babies. A banner, announcing the meeting, hung from the roof of a temple in the compound. A few temple-goers stopped by to listen to the conversations.

The meeting followed a pattern. The older members who were in-charge started with a primer on the Act and a quick revision of the rules—this was for parents who were new to the committee. Then a list was made of matters that needed immediate attention and intervention—a toilet needed repair in some school; midday meals were not regular in another, a boundary wall had to be made in the third and so on and so forth. These matters, I was told, would be taken up either by the SMC or the federation at the block and district; it depended on the level at which it could be solved.

What stood out was that this federation of SMCs included even those parents whose wards had moved on. This, Sanjay explained, was for the simple reason that some of these parents were very well versed with the Act and a huge asset in steering forward the SMC and federations. Though this is a deviation from the RTE Act, which only includes parents of current students in the committee, it is a very good idea.

The meeting, which had its agreements and disagreements, reached a feverish pitch towards the fag end when a few parents thought that it was the opportune time to barge into the office of the block education officer that very day to demand solving a long-standing matter. However, others thought differently. A logical and more strategic plan was drawn. The animated discussion was proof that regular trainings of SMCs had indeed empowered parents to take up issues on their own.

The wheels had been set in motion.

Parents Association…Where It All Began

Though SMCs, a community-based institution for monitoring RTE implementation, were made mandatory under Section 21 of the RTE Act, 2009, Lokmitra had already laid a strong foundation through its Parents Association in 2002. In fact, when the rules of the Act were being made in 2009, they were one of the key players pushing for proper provisions related to SMCs and in December 2008, for pushing for its approval from the Parliament before it went into election mode.

This the co-founders of Lokmitra, Rajesh Kumar and Priya Bharti attribute to the years of working at the grassroots and working with some of the best minds in education such as Vinod Raina and Professor Krishna Kumar. The 18 years that Oxfam supported them—first through Novib and then through Oxfam India—gave them a strong foothold in education.

The couple came from Bihar to Raebareli in the 1990s. They worked on women empowerment, labour rights, maternal and child health, education for out-of-school girls and local self-governance. The strand of work on education was still in its formative stage. It was while working with the brick kiln workers, who were mostly migrants, that the two realised that if parents could come together for their rights, they could surely be brought together for the rights of their out-of-school children.

Thus came about the idea of Parents Association. Parents were brought together and mobilised according to clusters and blocks and not on the basis of their schools, as was to later become the structure under the RTE Act. Stress was laid on bringing on board parents from the marginalised section, especially women. With this began Lokmitra's journey to boost their education profile. This was in 2002.

Now, before the RTE version of SMCs, was the Basic Siksha Adhiniyam's Village Education Committee (VEC). This was a committee comprising *Gram Pradhan* as the chairperson, senior-most teachers (head teacher) from all schools in that gram panchayat as secretaries and three parents nominated by the education officer or the head teacher. This committee, by its very structure, had zero accountability; only those parents who were in the good books of the officers made it to the committee. More parents needed to be a part of this to feel and be empowered. Hence, the Parents Association.

This work on Parents Association was instrumental in bagging the Oxfam Novib project, which they got despite falling short on the budget requirement of the project. "We had a couple of days for submitting the concept note. For the project, one of the criteria was that the NGO should have a budget of ₹50 lakh but we were falling short—our budget was just ₹22 lakh. But we were still selected. This was in 2003." Lokmitra's association with Novib, through the project, started in January 2004. The project was in Rahi and Salon block in Raebareli and Lalganj in Pratapgarh district.

In the first year, the focus was on the mobilisation of parents to take ownership of their children's education. They were federated at the block level and regular meetings were held. It was during these interactions that a need for grassroots intervention was felt. And so in 2005, the concept of Parents Association was taken at the school level. As was expected, entry into the schools was tough; teachers resisted this idea and considered outside intervention adversarial.

This is where the cluster level associations were useful. They held meetings and trained parents. Most importantly, they convinced the teachers that they were there to work with them and not against them. "The association received a vote of confidence from the teachers when the members rallied to demand for appointment of teachers in Dih. Dih had very few teachers," recalls Priya. In fact, over the years, the teachers' unions, who have their own administrative issues to deal with, have supported Lokmitra in their demands for quality education. "It is not that they do not want quality education but they have their own administrative issues to deal with. They trust us enough to have given their letterhead to endorse our work," says Sanjay.

In 2005, when the first draft of the RTE Act was out, they were quite thrilled to see a reference to SMCs. And since states had to decide on their own rules, Lokmitra has been one of the key players in advocating for robust SMC rules. At it wasn't just in the beginning, it continued till 2013 when Sharda represented SMCs in Lucknow. And the advocacy continued in different forms and shape. There were sit-ins, state consultations, rallies, talks with state bureaucrats and officers in the Centre (sometimes simultaneously) and a lot of interaction with educationists.

In fact, the relationships that they forged with educationists is reflected in the number of books on pedagogy and teaching methodology, from writers across the world and in different languages, stocked in their office library. "We had more time earlier. Now though it is a little difficult to sit and read, we know where to find the relevant information," chuckles Priya. It is this insatiable hunger for learning and experimenting with education that gave Lokmitra a strong foundation in pedagogy.

It was during the Novib partnership when they trained in pedagogy and later experimented with out-of-school adolescents. Nearly 500 adolescents were brought to a residential camp and were taught a syllabus based on the oral language experience. This meant using the words and the local dialect of the children in school and integrating them into the syllabus. Supplemented by other funding agencies, they tried formalising the system by providing supporting material for teachers and translating the existing books into a simple language (so that the material remained the same for out-of-school children as well as the regular school goers). At the end of the four-month camp, they were able to send nearly 250 children to school.

The basic premise of Lokmitra's pedagogy was using simple language—mother tongue. And the virtue of integrating the mother tongue with the regular Hindi and English was evident as we travelled south to Odisha, another one of Oxfam India's focus state.

Kulay and Birsa

Kulay Singh Sundhi, a 24-year-old man, is surrounded with kids waiting for their *Saar* to give his undivided attention to them. As soon as he turns to them, the students, from classes one to three, in their white and blue school uniforms, standing in a semicircle, break into a poem.

The poem goes thus, a *kulai* invited to eat food is asked to sit on a chair and, as soon as he sits, the chair breaks and he falls. This is a cue for all the children to jump and squat. The room is filled with peals of laughter. The children are thrilled and so is the teacher. He quickly turns around to explain. "This is a tiger," he says, as he shows us the play card. "Also called *bagho* in Odia and *kulai* in Ho. But when we teach our children, we start with *kulai*, then *bagho*, and then 'tiger'". Therefore, the *kulai* poem!

What seems like a simple rearrangement of words is actually what has brought back kids from the Ho community to the Bandhasahi New Primary School in Mayurbhanj's Kaptipada block. Charts of alphabets and numbers, names of fruits and vegetables, birds and animals—in Ho and in Odia—brighten up the classroom. The Ho tribes speak the Ho language.

This is what Multilingual Education (MLE) looks like. Simply put, schooling starts in the mother tongue, like Ho (in this case), and then after a couple of classes, moves on to additional languages like Odia (in this case), and then finally, to English or Hindi. Considering the rich diversity of language India has, this seems like the most logical thing to do. Odisha alone is home to 62 Adivasi groups and 29 Adivasi languages.

Article 350A of the Indian Constitution too talks about 'providing adequate facilities for instruction in the mother-tongue at the primary stage of education to children belonging to linguistic minority groups'. Yet this is not followed, as it should be. The impact is considerable though—the students are more confident, they are learning, they are coming to school and more importantly, they are staying in school.

Not far from Bandhasahi is Haldishahi Upper Primary School. And the scenes are similar, just with another teacher. The only difference is that Birsa Singh Biroli, a *Bhasha Sikshak* just like Kulay, was among the 3,500 MLE teachers recruited by the state; this was following a notification in 2014. Both Kulay and Birsa were two of the *Bhasha Sikshaks*—an MLE teacher—appointed by Sikshasandhan in 2011.

These teachers bridge the learning gap—nearly 23 per cent of Odisha's population is Adivasis and their literacy rate is 52.2 per cent (far below the state literacy rate of 73.5 per cent). The strategy is to start with the mother tongue in class one (in this case Ho), introduce Odia and English as subjects in class two and three respectively, while continuing with Ho or Santhali.

This makes the transition to Odia and English in the higher classes easier.

The Bandhasahi school was set up in 2010 and though it was close to the village, the attendance was dismal. For these Adivasi children, being taught in Odia was daunting. By his own admission, the headmaster-in-charge, Padmalocha Bhanja, said, "There was a language barrier. The teacher couldn't understand what the students were saying and vice versa. Parents couldn't follow what was being taught in school. Children used to come, eat and leave. Students of classes one to three were usually left to fend for themselves. Children were bound to drop out."

When I visited the school in 2014, Kulay's class and school had 100 per cent attendance; this was a massive turnaround from the 30 per cent before the language teachers were appointed to the school. Children had stopped coming to school and parents didn't engage through SMCs. The SMCs were at best non-functional and at worst non-existent!

The turnaround happened in 2013. And it wasn't overnight. Kulay's relentless visits to students' homes and talks with parents and children did the trick. Kuwar Jarika, an eleven-year-old boy from the Ho tribe, was one such potential dropout; he was in class three when he stopped going to a school in the neighbouring village. The distance was one reason but language was a bigger reason. The teacher taught only in Odia, a language Kuwar was not well conversant in.

After a few meetings with Kulay, the parents were convinced. "They were surprised and relieved that lessons would be in Ho and at a school so close to their home. When taught in their own language, they are not afraid of coming to school. There is this fear of an alien language," Kulay had said when we met in 2014.

A year of classes in Ho and some Odia helped Kuwar grasp basic concepts better. In 2014, he was in class five and was able to identify alphabets and numbers in English. Studies show that a child enrolled in class one, takes three years to understand either the textbook or the teacher. When the child cannot understand the language he/she is taught in, it makes the learning years difficult and this results in the highest number of dropouts in class two and three. Another study showed that both attendance and learning outcomes were better among tribal children who went to MLE schools. Kuwar is proof.

Languages carry culture. But it wasn't just the language that made the difference. "It was also about putting their culture in the heart of learning, and integrating Adivasi songs, stories, riddles and games in their curriculum," said Anil Pradhan, Sikshasandhan's member secretary. He was quick to add that it is also extremely important for the education system to align the school calendar according to their festivals. For instance, a *Maghe Parab* is of greater relevance to the Ho and some members of the Munda community than *Durga Puja*. Schools give holidays for *Durga Puja* and not *Maghe Parab*, but students take off for the latter, anyway. This leads to high rates of absenteeism.

Tribals are known for their love for festivals—"It spreads for over almost 10 days," Kulay smiled. "So while it is important to make changes in the calendar to ensure that children don't miss school, it is even more important to give them a sense of integration and importance," Anil said. We had met him at his second-floor office at Nayapalli in Bhubaneswar in 2014.

Palao Sunder Lagid

In Ho, *Palao Sunder Lagid* means, *Education for Change.* And this was the tagline for Project Birsa, the Oxfam India-Sikshasandhan project.

"Our back donors wanted to brand the project. And since we were trying to build the confidence and identity among tribal children through mother-tongue-based education, it was but natural that the project carried the name of their role model —Birsa Munda—and their language, hence Ho," said Anil.

But this could well have been the tagline for Anil—one of the founder members of Sikshasandhan. A soft-spoken man, Anil explained how the organisation, established in 1995, was built on the very premise of focusing and subsequently filling in the gaps in education in the state. Language, rather the medium of teaching, as it turned out, was the square peg in a round hole. From 1999, they began experimenting with language teachers through its Alternative Education Programme for Tribal Children. In the programme, teachers from the community taught children for a couple of hours in villages that had no schools and adopted a cultural curriculum.

The seeds of the idea of alternative education were sowed in a large consortium, led by Agragamee, in the early 1990s. Agragamee, a Rayagada-based NGO, was a pioneer in alternative education. The consortium was funded for watershed activities. An evaluation of the project showed that while these activities created economic opportunities, they were not sustainable. The lack of education marred their bargaining abilities and managerial skills.

Either there were no schools in these far-flung areas, or if there was one, there were no teachers. These assignments were often seen as punishment postings and they continue to be seen so! If there were teachers who did make it to the school, they taught in Odia and did not understand the tribal way of life. This was bound to have an impact on the children. The situation hasn't changed much since.

Soon after the implementation of the RTE Act in 2009, Sikshasandhan conducted a survey of out-of-school children in one of the gram panchayats in Mayurbhanj. This they did because they weren't too satisfied with the provisions in the Act vis-à-vis the tribal areas. They found 388 children were out of school. The government data showed just 5 children. And the reasons once again pointed towards the shortage of teachers and complete absence of tribal teachers. In 2011, before the start of Project Birsa, a baseline of the Noto Gram Panchayat showed that while there were 28 teachers appointed for these 11 schools, the remoteness of the schools meant high absenteeism and a subsequent impact on the nearly 1,000 students in these villages.

Anil's team has been relentlessly advocating with the state government for multilingual education and appointment of more teachers. In which they have had some success. In 2005, when the state government announced the introduction of English from class one, Sikshasandhan opposed. The member secretary shot of an article to *Odisha Bhaskar*, a daily, opposing the decision. When he met the editor to submit his article, he was told that they had already written an editorial supporting the government's stand but the paper, nevertheless, agreed to publish the article for the sake of a larger debate. The government then held a number of hearings and debates. And finally, the proposal was dropped.

The government, has over the years, tried some stopgap arrangements like translation of books in different Adivasi languages. This, Anil opposes. "It is more important to have language teachers. Mere translation of the text, without contextualisation, will not help if the teachers aren't trained in the language." Years of advocacy with the state government meant that the state was kept on its toes. They were made aware of the lacunae, of the gap that was leaving a large chunk of its population behind.

By 2007, the state had incorporated MLE in the Sarva Siksha Abhiyaan (SSA)—the first five years of schooling would be in the mother tongue—and initiated mother-tongue-based MLE in 10 languages in 545 schools with 384 MLE teachers and 428 *Siksha Sahayaks.* But there was a lot more that needed to be done. There were after all 11,497 schools!

A 2014 notification on MLE was much more exhaustive; 3,500 teachers were recruited. On paper, the government seems to be giving it full backing but the implementation is not as good as it should be. "In the government, everything depends on the commitment and understanding of the head of departments. Secretary changes, priority changes." The good thing, however, is that now there is a policy to hold the government accountable to!

But the one bureaucrat he very fondly speaks of is Rajesh Pravakar Patil, the district magistrate and collector of Mayurbhanj, who joined in 2012. He was keen to understand the Oxfam-Sikshasandhan project. Impressed, he went ahead and replicated the MLE model in 176 schools in the most remote areas of the district. This was a huge boost to Sikshasandhan's work.

Backed by its years in advocacy and riding high on the Mayurbhanj model, in 2013 Sikshasandhan became one of the members of the committee drafting the MLE policy. With its foot firmly in the power circuits, Anil and his team were able to convince the secretary of School and Mass Education that recruiting teachers from the tribal communities would solve the language problem of the children.

This level of advocacy, Anil feels, was possible because of Oxfam's partnership. They had pretty big funders backing them in the past. But Oxfam funded the project to some of the more inaccessible parts and supported in creating evidence for advocacy. Moreover, it helped establish and coordinate the Odisha RTE Forum, which has over the years become a major influencer.

Looking back, NGOs such as Agragamee and Sikshasandhan should get credit for keeping the government on its toes on the issue of multilingual education and alternative education. The state MLE policy now includes 21 languages.

Palao sunder lagid, indeed!

The Wrestlers of Hamirpur

MAN: "It's better to teach girls. It is better to send them to school."

I: "You think so?"

MAN: "The whole village thinks so."

I: "Why?"

MAN: "The boys are useless. The girls have made us proud."

I: "How?"

MAN: "Have you heard of Sakshi Malik?"

(Sakshi is the wrestler who won a bronze in the 2016 Olympics)

I: "Yes, I have."

MAN: "We have a couple of Sakshis in our village. And they have done us proud at the state level."

This was a surreal conversation. 'Send girls to school', 'they have done us proud'—these are not words one often hears and definitely not in a remote village in Uttar Pradesh's Hamirpur district. This gentleman had followed us to the girls' primary school in Sikhrodi village, which we were visiting in 2016, and insisted on speaking with us.

It turned out he was one of the SMC members and though his daughter was not a wrestler—he was proud of her nevertheless—she was on the kabaddi team. She was part of the district team that reached the final of the regional sports meet. Hamirpur had lost to Banda, a neighbouring district in the Bundelkhand region, in the finals. "But they had older and senior girls. That wasn't right. Otherwise, we would have defeated them," chipped in Preeti. She was one of the girls on the team. The boys had lost in the qualifying rounds.

Sikhrodi village is in the middle of a scrub forest far removed from any other village in the gram panchayat. The two approaching roads to the village were unmetalled and all mud, stone and dust. The village is dominated by the Kewat (boatmen) community; an OBC community who now also pursue farming (apart from being boatmen). Durgesh Chand of Samarth Foundation, who accompanied us, explained that children here were usually pulled out of school to support the parents in farming or other household chores. School wasn't really a priority.

Bundelkhand has had a long history of drought. The communities are vulnerable due to their dependence on agriculture and this, particularly between 2000 and 2010, led to rising levels of farmer distress, poverty, farmer suicides and out-migration. And around 2008–09, Devendra Gandhi was working on the implementation of one of the drought response programmes of the government. This took him to drought-affected villages, where he saw children sitting hungry and starved. Though he was working in the development sector and had been in similar situations in the past, this year turned out to be the tipping point for him.

Two things were clear, he says. While the men migrate in search of jobs, it is the women, children and elderly who are left behind to deal with abject poverty, hunger and at times, starvation. And second, children were more often than not pulled out of school; with no money and no food at home, children had to pitch in so that they could help in whatever income generation that was possible. "Something needed to be done about their education". He went ahead and set up Samarth Foundation.

And in 2013, Oxfam India began supporting Samarth in 19 gram panchayats of Kurara and Maudaha blocks of Hamirpur district. The underlying premise was to create a child-friendly environment in schools. They had their SMCs and Bal Sansads, but sports was among the most effective practices of getting children to school. And children such as Preeti were proof.

The school that we were in was one of the many schools that Devendra's Samarth Foundation got up and running. This primary school is usually referred to as 'Komal's school'. Komal is one of the wrestlers the 'man' spoke of. We were waiting for students to join us—it was well past their school time, so they were trickling in at their own pace. Durgesh meanwhile tells us how until a few years ago this school was mostly used as a storehouse. A teacher would come but there would only be a couple of students.

So first, the school was cleared. Then the challenge was to get the girls to school. Devendra recalls that the resistance from parents usually said, "हम बच्चों का पेट पालें, या उन्हें पढ़ाई के लिए भेजें।" ("*Should we feed the kids, or send them to school.*") This was a girls school and girls are usually pulled out of school to take care of siblings, while the parents go out to work—either as day labourers or migrant labourers. But they came around, once the children were convinced.

In order to convince children, who had been out of school for quite some time and hence unsure of how they would handle studies, Samarth assured them that sports is what they were keen on. They started with Ludo and carom board. "Through these we reintroduced simple maths to the students," recalls Devendra. Then team sports like kabaddi and kho-kho were introduced. "We needed more students for sports. So we got some of the boys—their school was outside the village—to this school. First, it was to play sports and eventually we made them attend classes," he chuckles. In a couple of months, the number swelled to over 25.

Finally, the kabaddi team arrived—Preeti, Anita, Ragini, Hitanshi, Chitra and Sampat with their certificates and mementoes, carefully wrapped in plastic packets. We were still waiting for Sadhna and Komal. They were the wrestlers. They were the 'Sakshi Maliks' the gentleman was talking about.

Not only has sports ensured that these girls remain in school, it has also helped smash some of the deepest patriarchal social norms one at a time. For the village, sending girls to a school was one thing but sending them for a sports meet to the block headquarters at Kurara was quite another. At first, the parents refused. So Samarth took them along. "That was important. When they saw their daughters perform so well, they were filled with pride. The next time there was a sports meet, they were more than happy to let the girls go," Durgesh says.

The girls made their parents realise that they were better than boys. They made the village realise that sports was something that girls could participate in and excel. And that they could be wrestlers!

Komal and Sadhna finally arrived and they barely looked like wrestlers. They had joined a secondary school in the neighbouring village when we visited them in 2016 but they continued to come here once in a while for practice. The interesting tidbit is that the two became wrestlers on a whim. They went as part of the kabaddi team at the district games in 2015 but were so captivated by the wrestling match that they decided to give it a shot. For girls to participate in combat sport without any prior training was a huge step. But they participated and won. They won at the regional level as well—Komal came first, Sadhna second. At the state level, Komal came second. She lost because she wasn't aware of all the manoeuvres and techniques. "But I am better prepared this year," Komal had said in 2016.

Komal and others like her realise the importance of school and sports. And they are shining examples of how far a little guidance can go in grooming young children. In their new schools, in the neighbouring village, they have set up a *Siksha Sahyog Kosh* or Education Support Bank, informs Devendra. This bank gives out stationery such as rubbers, pencils, pen, and notebooks. Students drop out of school if they do not have the basics; this bank ensures that no child drops out due to the lack of basic stationery. This is run by a few students who collect money—their pocket money, money from family they would have received during festivals, and contribution from the teachers and Samarth—and ensure that the bank is well stocked.

Back in 2016 itself, the girls are fairly well known in the state school sports circuit. They wanted to continue with their sports. They had already outperformed the boys. "We will train harder. We want to excel like Sakshi Malik," Komal had said.

Durgesh recalls that when they had first come back with a prize, the *Pradhan* (village head) was indifferent to their achievements. "'Sports, so what?' he had asked. He realised its significance when the district magistrate came to the school and felicitated the girls in front of the village. This meant a lot and helped change things around here," smiles Durgesh.

That surreal conversation was possible due to the change Durgesh talks about. And going by what the gentleman, we met earlier, had to say, the girls—rather the children of that village and all those villages that Samarth have taken sports to—seem to be in for the long run.

तेरे माथे पे ये आँचल बहुत ही खूब है लेकिन
तू इस आँचल से इक परचम बना लेती तो अच्छा था।

—**Asrarul Haq Majaz,** 'Naujawan Khatoon Se'

The title of the poem is 'Naujawan Khatoon Se'—the poet, Asrarul Haq Majaz, is addressing young women and he says: "You look quite dignified when you cover your head with your stole. But if you had turned your stole into a flag (to declare your independence from social rigidities), it would have been even better!"

Ending Violence Against Women
Uttar Pradesh, Odisha, Andhra Pradesh, Gujarat
2009–14

Violence Against Women (VAW) is one of the most widespread, and yet, the least recognised of human rights violations across the world. It manifests in the form of sex-selective abortions, early marriages, female genital mutilation, rape, sexual assault, dowry murder, honour killings and domestic violence, which is also one of the most pervasive forms. VAW continues to be a tool for individuals, societies and states to retain power over women, their labour, reproductive rights and their choices, preventing their participation as active citizens. It is thus one of the key aspects of social exclusion for women across the world.

From 2009 to 2014[1], Oxfam India implemented a multi-state project on addressing violence against women. The specific focus was to ensure the effective implementation of the Protection of Women from Domestic Violence Act (PWDVA), 2005, which was then a relatively new Act.

OIN implemented this programme across five states[2] by engaging key stakeholders to address domestic violence. The project was multifaceted. One of the key interventions was to demonstrate, scale and institutionalise the women support centres as an effective redressal model to respond to women facing domestic violence. The Oxfam India model of the women support centres was adapted from the model

---

[1] In 2009, Oxfam India was part of a consortium of seven United Kingdom-based International NGOs, with the support of Department for International Development (DfID), to implement the International NGOs Partnership Agreement Programme (IPAP). IPAP was a five-year programme from 2009 to 2014 on social exclusion where Oxfam India worked towards addressing violence against women (VAW).

[2] Uttar Pradesh, Bihar, Jharkhand, Odisha and Chhattisgarh.

developed by Tata Institute of Social Sciences (TISS) who referred to these as Special Cells for Women and Children.

Though the police-station-based women support centres were an integral part of the International Partnership Agreement Programme (IPAP) project, there was a need to look at ending violence against women in a more holistic way. While the police-station-based support centres were important, there was a need to reach out to women to define domestic violence for them. Physical abuse is the only one that women very clearly recognise as violence. They do not see mental, emotional, sexual or economic abuse as domestic violence. Since they do not recognise domestic violence, they also do not know how to deal with it? Who should they go to? What is the Protection of Women of Domestic Violence Act?

A community outreach was required and grassroots organisations became a necessity. They established counselling centres, gave women the courage to come out with their problems and ultimately enabled them to unite against oppression and abuse.

The project had several strands of excellent work by different NGOs. It wasn't possible to include each one of the partners so this story looks at a couple of broad themes of community outreach and women support centres. While the project had wins like institutionalising the women support centre, what the project very successfully managed to do was boost the confidence of women to demand justice for themselves and for others.

To End Violence Against Women

Left to Die

Sultana came out of coma after 21 days. She was in a general ward at the government hospital in Hyderabad. All she could recall of the moments before passing out was that her husband hit her with a big stone and he wouldn't stop and that there was blood splattered all over the room.

"It has been 15 years but I can still taste the blood and hear myself shout for help."

I met Sultana at Shaheen Women's Resource Centre in November 2017. She is one of the counsellors who work with Dalit and Muslim communities on domestic violence and inform them about PWDVA. "Women don't understand domestic violence. If a girl child is denied food or education; if a woman is not allowed to work and have a source of income; if the husband taunts and mentally tortures the wife, that is domestic violence."

Sultana's voice is calm and reassuring. Her calmness belies her past but her face is the constant reminder of the violence she suffered at the hands of her husband. After she had passed out on the floor of her house, her husband got a kitchen knife and slashed her nose and mouth. The last attack left her disfigured.

Back in 2002, she was 18 years old and heavily pregnant. Her neighbours rushed her to the hospital and called the police. Over the span of the next seven months, her life went through the wringer—she delivered a baby boy, was deserted by her husband, lived with her brother, left his home, stayed at Osmania hospital doing odd jobs and tried to commit suicide thrice.

Jameela Nishat, the founder-director of Shaheen, met Sultana at the hospital. "She was very comforting. She told me I was strong and brave and that I needed to live for my son. She got me a sewing machine and convinced my brother to keep me."

In 2005, she visited Jameela again; this time at the Shaheen Resource Centre. "Jameela *apa* asked me to join the centre. They trained women sewing, etc. But what was more interesting was that they were giving legal counselling as well as training on law." Sultana decided to take her husband to court.

Recounting her visits to the police station, Sultana says, it was unnerving. "They said that I must have been sleeping with another man. They also said that why I didn't come immediately after the incident. It was their mistake. They never came to the hospital to take my statement. On the other hand, they let my husband go, who ran away to Mumbai and married another woman."

She continues, "The woman is always accused of having instigated the man. They don't want to file a case citing it as a family matter, which shouldn't be brought out in public. At every stage, she is made to feel guilty while the perpetrator of violence goes scot-free. Plus, she gets no support from the community or the family. And so women simply suffer for the rest of their lives."

Sultana, Shaheeda, Archana—all counsellors—and I are in the courtyard of Shaheen's office at Baqshi Bazaar in Old Hyderabad. Women keep walking into the front office for counsel. Jameela *apa,* as she is fondly called, patiently hears out everyone who comes in. In the back are training rooms for sewing, knitting and computer classes. Another couple of rooms serve as a temporary shelter home. A staircase on the side of the courtyard leads to a terrace, which at times serves as the venue for workshops and trainings.

Baqshi Bazaar used to be a communal tinderbox in the 1980s and 1990s. The home that houses the centre had been abandoned after people were murdered and the house set on fire during riots. Jameela started the centre in 2002 as a response to the communal violence in Gujarat.

Reaching Out

It is from here that Shaheen Resource Centre began working on gender, skill development and violence against women. Jameela and her counsellors are the bridge between the survivors of domestic violence and the police, providing medical and legal aid. “But we didn’t simply start with talking about violence. We first set up a dispensary. Women used to come with stomach pain but they turned out to be cases of domestic violence.”

To reach out to young girls, they started English learning classes and skill centres. “On one occasion when we spoke of sexuality, 45 out of 50 girls left. The five teenagers who remained became our counsellors,” says Jameela.

The counsellors are the ears and eyes for the centre. They visit the houses in the colonies and the slums they work in, check on every house, tell them about their work and give them a booklet about the organisation. “Not everyone is ready to talk at that time. Some ask the girls to come back later. Some say nothing then, but call up the number that is given on the booklet. This is how women and young girls reach out to us.”

For Jameela and her counsellors, it hasn't been easy working in a Muslim area and talking about issues related to mobility and economic empowerment, or for that matter, encouraging women to go to the police instead of following what's there in the *Sharia.* Their office has been vandalised, their counsellors arrested, drunk men have gheraoed the centre and a *fatwa* has been issued against Jameela. "It was impossible for them to understand that a woman could run an organisation. They resented the fact that *hum unhe* road *dikha rahe the* (we were showing them the road)." The road being a reference to mobility.

Despite being called *talaq ghar*—for breaking families by encouraging women to speak up against violence—the centre doesn't rush to the police station at the very first instance. "We do a lot of counselling. We listen to the woman/girl, what action she wants to take. Not everyone wants to separate or file a case against the husband. If the woman/girl just wants her husband/father/brother counselled, then we do that. It is her decision that we support till the end," says Jameela.

Oxfam India implemented a programme—IPAP—from 2009 to 2014 with the specific focus to ensure the effective implementation of the PWDVA. In Andhra Pradesh, there were three gender partners among whom three strands of work were divided—counselling, police-station-based women support centres and research and advocacy.

Of the three, Shaheen Resource Centre focussed on counselling. While counselling was good, Jameela also offered to teach new skills at her centre so that chances of earning a livelihood were better.

Ram or Durga

For women to come out of domestic violence, it is first important to recognise it. I was visiting Dhenkanal in Odisha in 2014 to meet Pushpanjali Jena and Bhanu of the Indira Social Welfare Organisation (ISWO) one of our gender partners. We stopped at a meeting at one of the villages; it was at the panchayat hall. A young girl, whose name I regrettably forget, was leading the meeting from ISWO and she was talking to a young group of women about the PWDVA. At the close of the meeting, songs were sung and a pledge was taken to fight violence against women.

Just before the crowd began to disperse, one of the women asked, "But what about what happens at the government and private hospitals?" Everyone nodded and agreed something should be done. They were talking about a health centre about 15 km from the village.

The woman explained, "The health centre is in a nexus with the private nursing homes. They violate the sex determination law." Pre-natal sex determination has been banned in India since 1994, yet it goes on. This is how it worked at the health centre—when a pregnant woman went to the government facility for a check-up, she was referred to a private nursing home or at least given an option to go. At the nursing home, the woman was checked in the presence of her relatives. The examination room had two pictures on either side of the examination table—one of Ram and the other of Durga.

The doctor doesn't explicitly say if it's a boy or a girl. Instead, they just tip their head towards the pictures on the wall—Ram for a male foetus and Durga for a female foetus. If the head tip is towards Durga, more often than not, the family gives a subtle go-ahead to abort the child.

"Isn't this violence against women?" the women present in the meeting ask.

This wouldn't have been possible a few years ago, says Bhanu. From not knowing anything about domestic violence to calling out female foeticide, these women have come a long way. Credit for this goes to grassroots activists like Pushpanjali and Bhanu who have worked among the rural women for many years now, talking to them about gender-based violence, fighting against liquor and providing skill training.

ISWO trained women and men from rural communities to take discussions on violence against women to the villages. They are community mobilisers. They hold meetings to discuss the different aspects of domestic violence, the stakeholders and systems the aggrieved women have access to.

These meetings are open to men and women. "Domestic violence will never stop if we keep talking to women alone. These meetings have helped men and women to come to the women support centre," says Bhanu.

The community mobiliser is the link between the community and the police station. ISWO runs the women support centre at the SP office in Dhenkanal. Though they ran their support centre prior to Oxfam's partnership, under the partnership, they shifted to the SP office and their counsellors were trained at TISS.

Pushpanjali, one of the founding members of ISWO, mentions a rising number of cases at the support centre between

2009 and 2014. She explains that the cases of violence haven't increased, it is just that women and their family members have become more aware and are prepared to take action instead of suffering it.

When a woman reaches out to the community mobilisers and the vigilance committees in the villages (formed to keep an eye on the cases of violence and usually the first port of call), she is counselled. Even if she returns satisfied with the counselling, ISWO follows up on her case to make sure she is okay.

"In case there is no chance of an agreement, we begin counselling at the support centre," says Bhanu. The police too send cases to the support centre, where they think filing a case would be unnecessary. Migration is high. So apart from cases of domestic violence and dowry harassment, the women support centre receives several cases of trafficking, sexual harassment, molestation and child marriage.

ISWO shares a very good working relationship with the police department. Working together—police sitting through some of the counselling sessions and the counsellors attending some of the crime meetings—has ensured that both are sensitive to each other's scope of work, strengths and weaknesses. If the police consider a case sensitive, they send it to the women support centre and if the counsellors at the support centre want to summon an errant partner, they take the help of the police.

Bhanu recalls a case where the husband not just physically abused the wife but also kept all her degrees so she could not apply for a job elsewhere. She did not want a case, just her certificates back. The support centre called her husband for a counselling session but he didn't turn up. Finally, after the third notice, the police went and picked him up.

At the Police Station

Girija D Boddupalli, like Sultana, echoes the sentiment that women don't like approaching the police.

"They are not very comfortable. But when it is critical, they do go to the police station. So it was important that there is a support centre within the police station to counsel women and their families." Girija is the programme director of the Sakhi Centre in Telangana. She was a project officer at the Hyderabad office of OGB from 2003 to 2010 and was instrumental in bringing the idea of the police-station-based support centre to Oxfam in erstwhile Andhra Pradesh.

Girija, like Bhanu, agrees that police-station-based support centre works well but back then, in 2003 she wasn't sure, how. It was only after she saw a support centre in Mumbai being run on the TISS model that she was convinced.

TISS has been the pioneer in setting up the Special Cells for Women and Children; the first centre came up in 1984 (a collaboration between TISS and Bombay Police).[3]

But before it could become a part of IPAP, it was already up and running in Hyderabad. The OGB office roped in TISS in 2003. "A lot of lobbying and meetings were done with senior women IPS officers. TISS conducted trainings for the police

[3] https://www.tiss.edu/uploads/files/6Special_Cell_for_Women_and_Children_across_India.pdf

and for our partners. A lot of groundwork went in before we got the breakthrough," says Girija.

The first women support centre was set up at the Central Crime Station (CCS), next to the superintendent of police office in Basheerbagh, in 2004. "Initially, we weren't too happy. We would have wanted it in the commissioner's office but we realised that only the very serious cases go there. The CCS, on the other hand, had 31 police stations under it and would get almost 30 cases a day."

Oxfam's gender partner, Society for Women's Awareness and Rural Development (SWARD), a Medak-based NGO, managed the support centre; the counsellors were trained by TISS. SWARD was given a very small space but they built their credibility through their work. "Sivakumari's commitment to the cause and the spirit to fight the system was commendable and it played a big role in the success of the CCS centre." Girija further adds that as word spread, the footfall at the centre increased and eventually SWARD got a much bigger space, with waiting area and separate counselling rooms, within the police station.

Backed by the success of this model, the women support centre was proposed when the IPAP proposal was being drawn up. The entire team was cognizant of the fact that if it were successful in one state, it wasn't necessary that it would be successful in the other. They were toying with the options of setting up the support centre within or outside the police station. Many brainstorming sessions later, it was decided to go with the police-station-based support centre.

But this wasn't cast in stone. The programme was very mindful of the fact that the police might not be supportive, equally, in all states or districts. In the case of Uttar Pradesh, while one of the partners, Sri Ramanand Saraswati Pustakalya (SRSP), promoted one police-station-based support centre in Azamgarh, the other partner, Vanangana in Chitrakoot, found it difficult to negotiate this space with the police. They ran the support centre outside of the police station.

The women support centre in the police station helped break the ice between the counsellors and the police. "They were very supportive. They really liked the idea of a police-station-based women support centre. In fact, they had agreed to invest in many such support centres through the state; they had to be shelved back after agitations demanding separate statehood broke out in erstwhile Andhra Pradesh," says Girija.

It picked up, though, after Telangana was formed in 2014. The support centre at CCS was still being operated by SWARD. The Hyderabad City Police launched their own support centre, Bharosa, in 2016; this was on the lines of the CCS centre run by SWARD.

Once Bharosa started operations, SWARD gradually had to leave. "Though it was a little sad, but this is what we had always wanted. We wanted the police to take up this model and run. They did it and that was our success," says Girija.

The Gujarat Model

While in erstwhile Andhra Pradesh, Hyderabad City Police picked up the model, in Gujarat it was institutionalised through the state. The police-station-based women support centre that started as a pilot in 2009, is now in all the 33 districts in the state.

In Gujarat, the setting up of the women support centres in the police stations required strategic and consistent advocacy and liaisoning with different state machinery especially the police (through the Home Department) and the Department of Women and Child Development. It took a year of persuasion, strategic meetings, advocacy and investment in resources and infrastructure by OIN and TISS in 2010.

Gujarat Police granted permission to initiate women support centres on a pilot basis in the state. Seven women support centres across the police stations were set up in seven districts of the state. OIN supported four partners: Ahmedabad Women's Action Group (AWAG), Area Networking and Development Initiatives (ANANDI), Saurashtra Kutch Network against Violence against Women (SKVAW) and Centre for Development to implement the women support centres.

Across the four states, OIN worked with gender partners who had significant experience of working on violence against women, existing interventions at the community level for women survivors and strong linkages with government departments. The counsellors were well trained by TISS and they were always kept up to date with refresher trainings.

The police department provided the necessary infrastructure and support. A separate area within the police station for the women support centres to provide a safe and confidential space for women survivors was also allocated. This was a significant win given the police stations were already facing space crunch for their staff!

The interest of the Gujarat Police in these support centres can be judged by the fact that they invited counsellors for building their capacities on issues of gender and violence against women. Between 2010 and 2013, OIN and TISS held a series of strategic meetings with different departments, especially Home and Women and Child Development, to explain the model and the need to institutionalise the model as a government programme.

A proposal was presented to the government to upscale these centres to all districts and blocks of Gujarat. The impact of the women support centres both for women survivors and for police stations was soon beginning to show. Media lauded the women support centre in Patan for establishing an effective model of partnership with the state.

Convinced, eventually, the state government accepted the proposal and invited OIN and TISS to facilitate the process of institutionalisation of the women support centres. On 8 May 2013, Anju Sharma, the then secretary of Women and Child Development of Gujarat announced the scaling up of women support centres by the state during the launch of 'Hand to Hold' (a booklet based on the experiences and learnings of the women support centres).

The women support centres, now called Police Station Based Support Centres (PBSC), would be housed with the Women and Child Development Department and anchored by the Gender Resource Centre (GRC).[4] GRC is the nodal agency to implement department schemes and programmes such as PBSC, 181 women helpline and State Resource Centre. PBSCs were initially scaled up in 26 districts and now they have been set up in all 33 districts of Gujarat. There are 35 PBSCs; one in each of the 33 districts of Gujarat and two additional at the block level.

When talks began, some of the major challenges identified in institutionalising women support centres were frequent transfers of supportive and sensitised officials, poor coordination among different departments of the state government and delays in responses by the departments.

After having run for a couple of years, Dinesh Kapadia, former director of GRC laid down a few challenges the PBSC was facing—inadequate remunerations for the counsellors and lack of space in police stations. The footfall in the support centres was increasing by the day and so a need to expand was felt especially at the block level to be able to reach out to women in the remote and marginalised areas.

The PBSCs were up and running when I visited Gujarat and specifically Godhara in November 2017. This was the only place in Gujarat, where both the support centres ran—one by the GRC and the other, originally there by ANANDI. "The GRC counsellors have resigned. The post is vacant for the last

[4] The GRC, established in July 2003, was instituted by Gujarat's Women and Child Development (WCD) Department to provide support for incorporating gender equity and equality in the overall development process and plans of the state.

eight months. The cases keep coming so I have been asked to continue," says Seema Joshi, ANANDI's counsellor posted at the Dahod Rural Police Station. The day I visited, there were two cases at the centre.

Seema counselled a young couple patiently. A lady police constable sat at the opposite end. Seema points out that in the pilot stage of the women support centre (which was run by Oxfam partners), there was a strong community base—Nyay Samiti—that proved a useful link between the community and the support centre as well as an important referral system. In cases of witch-hunting, gang-rapes and POCSO (Protection of Children from Sexual Offences Act, 2012), the Nyay Samiti was the preferred forum.

Seema says that even now if the government needs help in reaching out to the community or for support, they go back to the Nyay Samiti. "We continue to support the counsellors at GRC whenever they require any help."

Even after all these years, the enthusiasm in the NGOs that ran the pilot project is commendable. Perhaps what can make the state-run PBSC better is a monitoring committee of civil society that can provide strategic guidance and improve the implementation of these centres.

"*Chotta umare chotta umare na debe biha, suna baba o, chotta umare na debe biha.*"

("*I am young, I am young. Don't marry me off. Father are you listening, I am young, don't marry me off.*")

—**Suman**, explains in this song, in her Nagpuri dialect, the ills of child marriage, the impact on the physical and mental health of the young girls and subsequently on the newborn. She was a part of the adolescent girls' group in Jidu village in Ranchi's Ormanjhi block.

Improving Maternal Health Through
Social Determinants Approach
Bihar, Jharkhand, Odisha, Rajasthan,
Maharashtra and Chhattisgarh
2012–15

Back in 2009, India's Maternal Mortality Ratio (deaths per 1,00,000 live births) was 212—one of the highest rates of maternal deaths in the world.[1] Approximately 1.3 per cent of the GDP was spent on public health, which showed the glaring lack of focus on maternal health or healthcare for women before and during pregnancy, childbirth and postnatal phase.

As one travels to the remote villages, it isn't uncommon to find a primary health centre (PHC) lacking in even the barest minimum facilities—medicines and emergency kits, an ambulance service and roads that can bring the ambulance to the doorstep of a woman in excruciating labour pains. Frontline workers such as Accredited Social Health Activists (ASHA) are overburdened and fatigued. Doctors are more often than not missing and the nearest hospital with any facility worth mentioning is so far that the family cannot afford it.

In rural India, especially in the marginalised communities, women and girls have limited access to and availability of health services, safe institutional delivery, nutritious food, choice of contraception or the agency to plan their own pregnancy. There are strict limits on their freedom, agency and access to information. But most importantly, their health and well-being is not a priority. All these social determinants influence the health-seeking behaviour of women and their families. Along with infrastructure, this too required to change.

One would push the other. So keeping in mind the rights-based approach to health (universal access to healthcare), the

---

[1] https://www.livemint.com/Politics/3uK62sim31WSgbyB5Bw4AP/Indias-maternal-mortality-rate-falls-but-still-a-long-way.html

project—Initiative to Improve Maternal Health through Social Determinants Approach—was conceptualised.

The project planned to plug the gap between the demand and supply side factors and streamline the healthcare experience. The demand side was strengthened through the generation of awareness among the community, of their entitlements, such as the right to food, capacity building to claim those entitlements through food security committees, harnessing the strength of in situ change agents such as barefoot auditors and groups of adolescent girls and empowering the community institutions like Village Health Sanitation and Nutrition Committee (VHSNC) to sustain the change in long run. On the other hand, the supply side interventions focused on capacity building of the frontline functionaries such as ASHA and Auxiliary Nurse Midwife (ANM) and leveraging on the government programmes through closer interaction.

The project[2] was implemented during 2012–15 in six states—Bihar, Jharkhand, Chhattisgarh, Odisha, Maharashtra and Rajasthan.

---

[2] 'Improving Maternal Health in Six States of India' was conceptualised under the Global Poverty Action Fund (GPAF) with support from the Department for International Development (DfID). GPAF focused on poverty reduction and the pursuit of Millennium Development Goals (MDGs) through improved service delivery, empowerment and accountability, work on conflict, security and justice.

Making Maternal Health Matter

Let's Talk About Sex

Dashrathi Mullick was taken aback when asked if he would undergo the operation instead of his wife. The discussion, one afternoon in Phulbani block in Odisha's Kandhamal district, had veered towards family planning and contraception. He was hesitant for a split second. But a little prod from his colleague, Mamta Digal, and the fact that he acted in a short film on vasectomy, and he conceded.

"अगर बीवी बोलेगी तो करवा लूँगा।"

"*If my wife says, I will get it done.*"

Dashrathi's commitment, or rather comment, was progressive. All things considered. While Odisha scored well on awareness regarding contraception (NFHS-III), it was female sterilisation that was more popular. Vasectomy was considered taboo because there was a strong belief that the procedure would make the man weak and render him unacceptable to the gods (after he died, of course).

This was in 2014 and Oxfam India (OIN) was just about wrapping up a six-state project that aimed at improving reproductive health. But it wasn't about just looking at whether PHCs worked or whether they had the facilities to deliver services. The approach was more holistic.

Institutional structures to ensure community-based monitoring of health services (such as Gaon Kalyan Samitis, which were village-level committees responsible for health, sanitation and nutrition) and food distribution (food security committees to ensure the steady supply of rations were formed) were put in place. Barefoot auditors were selected from within the community to keep the village informed about Kishori Kalyan Samitis, that is, groups of adolescent girls were formed to give them a platform to discuss issues of health, sanitation, nutrition and child marriage. In fact, a few firebrand members of the Kishori Samitis called off their own marriages as they were yet to turn 18, the legal marriageable age.

In a nutshell, the project looked at all the social aspects of maternal health and subsequently, the health of the child—contraception, birth spacing, institutional delivery, child marriage, nutrition and antenatal care (ANC).

It was about getting the community to talk about it. And talk it did. A few like Dashrathi were beginning to talk about, and acknowledge, male contraception. This, one might say, was one of the successes of the project. But this took a couple of years and some innovative outreach plans.

Condoms and birth pills were made available on *Mamta Diwas*. But since this was one of those women-only days, men, much to their convenience, stayed out of it, thus, the impact was negligible. 'Convenience' because during one of the village meeting, a male member of the Gaon Kalyan Samiti said, "Maternal health is for women. It does not concern us." They seem to completely black out the little detail that they could have contributed to the pregnancy or that perhaps they should take up the responsibility of the health of the mother and the child. It is a mindset problem that a couple of years of conducting the project were unlikely to undo.

So men like Dashrathi were a ray of hope!

Keeping men out of the *Mamta Diwas* is a bad idea. Despite an impressive turnout of pregnant and lactating women on the day at Jhara Balaskumpa village, and a generous display of condoms and birth control pills at the *anganwadi* centre for the women to choose from, there were still a handful of thirty-year-olds with their fifth and sixth child on the way. Theoretically, contraception, especially the use of condoms, needs both men and women to be on the same page, with the same level of awareness and willingness. But in practice, the decision and willingness to use condoms lies entirely with men.

The way these programmes are laid out, it is impossible to change their fabric overnight. And OIN understood that there had to be another way to reach out to men. The meetings and structure of the various committees such as Gaon Kalyan Samitis, food security committees and Kishori Kalyan Samitis were made more inclusive. But a better, more forceful option had to be explored to drive home the point—that men were key players in ensuring maternal health—and make a dent in the patriarchal and archaic mindset.

Centre for Youth and Social Development (CYSD), Oxfam's partner for the project in Odisha, brainstormed on several ideas of experimenting with different mediums. It began with the suggestion to use folk dance and music which graduated to making films. And then that went a step ahead and it was suggested making films with locals.

So a film with local actors was now in the works. A production house was bought on board, topics for films decided, scripts written, shooting locations identified and the hunt for local talent ensued. Many auditioned, few made the cut. All of them became celebrities in their own way; for a few, the stardom helped them to reach out to more and more people.

So we decided to reach out to a few of these 'stars' ourselves. Dashrathi was one of them. Martha Digal, an ASHA worker from Rajika Khol village in Kandhamal, was another. She is a health worker-turned-star. She has a kind smile and a genuine concern that reflects in her eyes; perhaps that is what makes her very popular as well.

We caught up with her during one of her rounds. The woman, at whose house we met, had just delivered her third baby at a PHC a few weeks ago. Martha had been counselling the couple to go for vasectomy or at least use contraception. "She is very weak," Martha said. Trainings and workshops brought out the leader in her and a campaigner for institutional delivery. She played herself in a film on institutional delivery—*Shaabash Amit* (Well Done Amit), and another on ANC—*Tini Parjaya* (Three Chapters).

But what makes her a fierce champion is also her lived experience—she was married at 15 and was a mother of three children by 30. "If I had access to information on birth spacing and contraception, I would have planned my pregnancies better." Between 2012 and 2015, she worked hard to ensure that her village had 100 per cent institutional delivery; there was no infant and maternal mortality or cases of malnourishment reported. She was popular and effective—the neighbouring villages requested her to visit them, her work had been documented and she has also been the recipient of the Best ASHA Worker Award from her district.

The films did many things. First, the films brought reproductive health to the discussion table—a table with both men and women at it. For one of the films on the nutritional needs of pregnant women, the cast was all male. In the film, the father agrees to give away the daughter only after the prospective groom is able to explain how he would take care of the nutritional needs when his daughter becomes pregnant.

This film showed that men needn't be shy about discussing pregnancies and the nutritional requirement of a pregnant woman. In fact, after the screening of this film, and by virtue of locals having acted in the film, these discussions became more commonplace at the Gaon Kalyan Samiti meetings. With more men understanding its importance and taking responsibility of their wives and children, the footfall in *Mamta Diwas* increased.

Two, the films helped bust myths. After watching *Mamta*—a film on anaemia and nutrition—a pregnant Manjula Kanhar stopped going for work that required her to dig pits through the day. Instead, she started going for regular check-ups, took rest and followed the iron-folic medicine regime on the advice of the ANM didi. The medicines were avoided because Manjula, like the rest of the villagers, believed would cause complications in pregnancy.

Third, the films proved to be an effective medium of learning. Apart from screenings, the actors themselves picked a thing or two. It was Dashrathi's stint as an actor, in a film on contraception, that the 35-year-old father of two is no longer averse to the idea of going under the knife.

Fourth, the films eased finding answers to uncomfortable questions. *Jagan Gaatha,* a film on contraception, was being screened at a house in Duti Mendi village; women and adolescent girls attended this. As expected, there were a few giggles, whispers and some awkward moments. But as soon as the screening was disrupted, due to power outage, the women and girls started discussing among themselves. Martha was there to chip in with some details but it became evident that some messages were conveyed better through films than just meetings.

And it is for this very reason that Martha, Mamta and Dashrathi feel that there should be a film that gives a blow by blow account of vasectomy and clears the myth around male sterilisation. "It should also explain the health impact of sterilisation on men and women. Only then perhaps there will be more takers for vasectomy. At the moment, it is almost nil," said Mamta.

The five Odiya documentaries took a year to get made. They were first screened in August 2014. By the end of the year, films were screened in 69 villages in Kandhamal and Sundargarh. The fact that actors were their neighbours and family, who in the course of acting picked up quite a bit, worked as an added advantage.

Harnessing the Power of Community

Around the time, that Odisha was planning films to broach issues regarding maternal health, Bihar was bracing up to start from scratch. The first step was getting the PRI (Panchayati Raj Institution) house in order, so to speak, that is, the VHSNC. In Bihar, this committee is made at the panchayat level and not at the village level but they were either non-existent or non-functional. The money allotted to these committees—₹10,000 annually—almost always lapsed. And if the committees ever used this money or were aware of its existence, maternal health was the last thing on their minds.

Pratiush Prakash who joined as a project officer after six months of the launch of the project had to run with it almost immediately. By the time he came, the NGO partners—Bihar Voluntary Health Association (BVHA) and Bihar Gram Vikas Parishad (BGVP)—had completed the baseline study.

The problem was loud and clear—early identification of pregnancy was a challenge. And this triggered a domino effect. ANC and postnatal care (PNC) regimes weren't followed, and this further increased the chances of casualties during delivery. The last bit was exacerbated by a number of reasons—not having money or the information of where institutional delivery can be done or the number of the free ambulance service. To add to it, poor road connectivity made the services even more inaccessible.

"We didn't know about the services, our rights or the precaution that we should take for pregnant women," Ram

Lakhan Yadav had said during a visit in 2015. He was from Runnisaidpur village in Sitamarhi.

In the mix of all this was the issue of community and caste dynamics, especially that of Dalits and Muslims. "Getting through to the Muslim communities, in Kishanganj, was the toughest. Initially, the sentiment was at best adversarial. There was no permission to meet with the women or girls, which meant that talking to them about maternal health would be impossible. With the Dalits the problem was their access to services," recalls Pratiush.

The work with the Dalits was in Sitamarhi. Here the *anganwadis* were in that part of the village where the upper caste lived; this made services inaccessible for Dalit women. To add to it, the distribution of the THR for pregnant and lactating women, under the Janani Suraksha Yojana, was limited to only eight women every month. In the absence of an active village-level committee, which could oversee the implementation of the scheme, the selection of these women was at the discretion of the upper caste *anganwadi* worker. With caste dynamics at play, Dalit women were always left behind.

It had to begin from scratch. Considerable effort was put in forming village-level VHSNCs (which was inclusive and which could feed into the panchayat-level committee), training them, creating awareness and building pressure on the public health services. This bore fruit.

The result of regular meetings and trainings was that the Dalits in Olipur and Sirsiya villages in Belsand block in

Sitamarhi campaigned for a mini *anganwadi* in a Dalit tola and got it. The community also proposed a rotation system so that more women could benefit from the 'eight women' cap for THR. This too was accepted.

Kishanganj had the worst Maternal Mortality Ratio of the three project districts. The third was Supaul. And the problem here was access to the community. The majority of Muslims in Kishanganj were from the conservative Shershahbadi community. The only possible access to the community was through religious leaders—the *mullah* and the *maulvis.*

"We started to involve them in our meetings. Heard their points of view, told them ours. It took nearly 8–10 months to convince them that our intention was to work with the community to improve maternal health status in these villages," says Pratiush.

And go to the community, they did.

In 2018, we met with Moeena Khatun. She was visiting her natal home at Harsadangi village. Now 22 years old, married for two years and with a child in tow, she was relaying the brick cook stove at her house. She takes a break; Moeena sits with us for a chat.

"I would see groups of 14–15 girls walk past the house. They seemed like they were going for a meeting. I also wanted to be a part of the group. I enquired and one of them took me along," she recalls. This was in 2013. Within a few meetings, she grasped the relevance of the committee, the meetings and the information that came out of these meetings. Stress was laid on preventing child marriage, ensuring health and hygiene, facilities at *anganwadi* centres and the monthly Village Health and Nutrition Day (VHND).

"I would be a mother too, someday. It was important for me to know about health and nutrition, institutional delivery, contraception and birth spacing. It was important that every girl knew about it," she says. She brought 20 other adolescent girls on board. She along with others like Nasira Khatun from Noniya Basti were at the fore of demanding the formation of a village-level committee.

If it was about health and nutrition, the ration distribution needed to be streamlined. So the girls went to the Public Distribution System (PDS) shop which was irregular in its distribution of ration. "In the beginning, he did not acknowledge us and asked 'Who has sent you?' 'Who are you?' Then we called a panchayat after which the PDS distributor apologised. He touched our feet and said he will never make this mistake again," says Nasira in a short documentary film *Finding One's Voice*. We couldn't meet Nasira in 2018.

The girls started monitoring the *anganwadi* centres—there was no sitting area or toilets. "We got toilets built," Moeena recalls her stint as the president of the committee. She is unable to do much in her marital village. She is married into a very conservative Shershahbadi family, where discussions on institutional delivery and contraception are considered 'dirty talk'. It was her stint with the committee that ensured her of a hospital delivery despite opposition from her in-laws. "I had kept the ambulance number handy," she smiles. With her experience of community-based monitoring and levels of awareness, she was offered the position of *anganwadi* worker.

While on our way back from Harsadangi village, we met Manzoor Alam. He had been the president of the committee in the past. He recollects how ₹70,000 (there were seven villages in Chakla Panchayat and each received ₹10,000) were spent to improve facilities for pregnant and lactating mothers. "'Purdah', an examination table and a bed was put up at all Health Sub Centres in the panchayat, so that check-ups could be done in privacy. A tank was built for water collection. Soaps were provided at each centre. Water coolers were placed in schools. Things had improved quite a bit back then," he says.

He rues the fact that after the Oxfam project ended, things didn't run as smoothly. "Perhaps a little more handholding was required," suggests Danish Meeraj of BVHA. It was clear that with support, communities could access their rights. In Bihar where caste takes precedence, tiding over differences and making transparency and accountability the key without losing sight of the larger picture of maternal health was commendable.

Singing Their Way Out of Child Marriage

Back in 2014, my former colleague Oommen C Kurian had just returned from his trip to Jharkhand. He was trying to upload a video of a seventeen-year-old Suman singing a song in the Nagpuri dialect. The song was:

> "Chotta umare chotta umare na debe biha, suna baba o, chotta umare na debe biha." (I am young, I am young

don't marry me off. Father are you listening, I am young don't marry me off.)

"Suman and other girls like her are singing the community out of child marriage," he had explained. He had met Suman at Jidu village in Ormanjhi block of Ranchi district.

My colleague described Suman as the 'celebrity crusader who pens and sings her songs in the local dialect to convince parents in her village of the ills of child marriage'. She also made her debut on the radio. This was quite remarkable considering girls from some of these villages never even got out of their homes. But Suman's popularity encouraged others to come out and perform at health *melas.*

Like in Bihar and Odisha, groups of adolescent girls were formed. Child marriage was the highlight of the project in the state because data showed that nearly 45 per cent women were married before they turned 18. The songs were an effective way of putting across their point. But the songs weren't limited to child marriage, they spoke of education, entitlements and the importance of health and proper nutrition for the mother and the child.

Adolescent girls group in Mukru village, like Suman's, had started a small savings fund. They deposited ₹5 every week from their pocket money. This was used to pay the registration fees for board exams for those who couldn't pay and were at the risk of dropping out due to lack of funds. This is a crucial step, considering Jharkhand is one of the worst-performing states on literacy.

So that was another hurdle for the project—an unlettered community. But the project devised a way to turn it on its head. Child In Need Institute (CINI) prepared illustrative Information, Education and Communication (IEC) material. A village health resource centre was set up which aggregated all the information on health and nutrition. It was a sort of library with posters and all possible material on health and nutrition of women and girls. There were charts and calendars prepared to keep a track of all pregnant and lactating women and their ANC and PNC regimes.

One interesting concept was *tiranga bhojan,* a list of food items that were essential to fight anaemia. Food, important for pregnant and lactating mothers, was divided into the three colours of the national flag. For instance, all food items such as milk and eggs fell in the white category; all green leafy vegetables represented the green; saffron stood for all ripe fruits and vegetables, meat and fish. These charts were put up at the resource centres and at *anganwadi* centres, and shared with all pregnant and lactating women.

As was in the case of Odisha, the project busted a few myths. The fact that colostrum (mother's first milk) was always avoided, changed. Also, the most common disinfectant used for the umbilical cord, after home deliveries, was cow dung. This often led to infection and death. That stopped as well. Within a couple of years in 2014, out of the 1,196 deliveries in all the 70 villages, skilled health personnel delivered 1,087.

Despite the fact that the project in Jharkhand had a few handicaps to begin with—such as PRIs were still in their very formative stage as the first panchayat elections in the state was held in 2010 and the low literacy rate—working with tribals was among the easiest as compared to the other marginalised communities like the Dalits and the Muslims. The acceptance of the project and the outcomes reinforced the need to work on maternal health.

Dead Women Talking

When Sanjeeta Gawri came back to Mumbai from Gadchiroli, she was unable to get any sleep. "Every time I shut my eyes, the dead women would start talking to me," she recalls. She was involved in Maternal Death Review (MDR)—a social autopsy of the death of women during pregnancy or after delivery.

The year was 2013 and Sanjeeta was the health and education officer in Oxfam India's Mumbai office; this office later moved to Raipur. The project was built around the underlying tenet 'Improving Maternal Health through Social Determinants Approach' so the parameters were institutional delivery, child marriage, contraception, ANC and PNCs, the health and nutrition committees and the health and nutrition days. MDR wasn't in the original scheme of things. Or in project-speak, 'in the log frame'.

The idea was triggered at a meeting organised by CommonHealth in Chennai in 2012. What piqued her curiosity was the fact that MDR was intrinsically linked to social determinants. A maternal death review was an opportunity to improve the quality of safe motherhood and prevent any future maternal and neonatal morbidity or mortality. The meeting at

Chennai spoke of social autopsy method to document these cases; these were 'interviews conducted to identify social, behavioural and health systems contributors to maternal and child deaths'.

"The MDR was the social autopsy that looked at these cases from the rights and gender lens rather than a clinical or biomedical angle. The end goal was the same—to improve safe motherhood," Sanjeeta recalls as we sat in her office in Delhi in 2019. So she floated the idea within the organisation. Usually, once a project is made, a log frame is set, a host of activities decided upon; it is almost impossible to make mid-course corrections.

So there was some resistance from the Delhi office before a go-ahead was given. The training was organised for all the partners in Bhopal in January 2013. But there was a second round of resistance. Social autopsy was an intensive, tedious and a soul-sapping process—finding out about a death, several rounds of questioning and interviews with the surviving family, checking health and medical records, verification, etc. The project was already well packed and the partners weren't sure if they had the bandwidth to carry out something like this. The social autopsy would have to be carried out along with other strands of work such as strengthening community-based monitoring as well as the VHSNCs.

So while the other states decided to not opt for it, Sanjeeta persisted with her Gadchiroli partner—Amhi Amchya Arogyasathi (AAA). She started accompanying the staff to the village to enquire about maternal death. She remembers her first meeting, when some very old cases of maternal deaths came up. "They have to be more recent or else the recall value is simply not there. Then we also realised that while on the one hand getting public records was difficult, whatever documents there were, were consigned to the funeral pyre with the dead woman."

The first meeting was sort of a trial run, which exposed the need for a better understanding of what accounted for maternal death. After a couple of such visits, it got better. The identification and documentation of MDR was much more streamlined. Seven cases were recorded in 2013 in the three blocks of Kurkheda, Korchi and Armori. By 2014, these numbers went up to 13. This wasn't comprehensive data by any stretch of the imagination; these villages were remote with no access to healthcare. Yet it was a start.

The deaths were gut-wrenching. But they were completely avoidable. One woman, four months into her pregnancy, died due to the wrong treatment for chickenpox by a quack. Had there been a doctor or a working PHC, she would not have had to go to a quack. Another woman died due to a delay in obstructed labour. She went into labour but her family couldn't arrange for an ambulance on time; when she was finally taken to the PHC, she was referred to the hospital due to complications. She finally died before she could reach the hospital. The lack of ANC and complications thereafter caused the death of a baby in the womb of another woman.

Lack of doctors in these far-flung areas or any semblance of a functional PHC had a serious impact on maternal health.

And these stories had to move beyond documentation. The project was built on the principles of transparency and accountability so a public hearing looked like the most logical next step. "Human lives had been lost due to the negligence of the system. And they deserved answers."

The public hearing was held in Gadchiroli on 18 February 2014, at the District Zila Parishad Hall. Local MLAs, members of the State Health Community Monitoring and Planning Committee members, district health officials and government doctors were present while family members gave their testimonies. While the families broke down recalling the causes of death, the health officials went on the back foot. The families spoke of doctors not paying attention and the lack of blood at the hospitals, on the other hand, doctors and health officials blamed everything from malaria to sickle cell anaemia for the women's death. But they did not accept their fault. There were a few doctors on the panel who did acknowledge that they were indeed short-staffed and doctors who were present at the PHCs and sub-centres weren't the most qualified.

"They started demanding documents and proofs. They tried to corner the families. They doubted our data collection, which was ratified by specialists. This was an eye-opener for all of us," says Sanjeeta. At this point, they realised how difficult it was to get records, either from the hospitals or from families. And it was because there were no maternal death reviews despite the guidelines of the National Health Mission. And this became the pivot for advocacy.

Goaded by the public hearing, AAA along with Oxfam conducted training on MDR for ANM, Accredited Social Health Activists (ASHA), *anganwadi* workers and all members of the VHSNCs. The district health officials were invited for these trainings. To make MDR a regular feature, AAA played a very pivotal role in following up and ensuring that MDR was done as mandated by the health policy.

What perhaps won the district officials was the realisation that Oxfam and AAA weren't adversaries. The latter acknowledged the problems faced by health workers, whether it was the lack of infrastructure or simply manpower. Thanks to the advocacy and constant follow-ups by the partner NGO at Gadchiroli, the district has taken up MDRs seriously. They inform those at AAA of all MDR cases.

"These went unreported because everyone from the ANM to the doctors wants to maintain an unblemished record. But unless one acknowledges the problem, they cannot solve it," Sanjeeta says. And this is what the district began to do. At least, took the first step—acknowledge it.

Anchoring the Project

In 1979, three young doctors, fresh from college, decided to start working among the excluded and marginalised communities. They were based out of a village called Devgarh, some distance away from the Choti Sadri block in Chittorgarh. Their focus was on health, and OGB, remembers Dr Narendra Gupta (one of the three), was their first funder. "Oxfam GB had their office in Ahmedabad. They supported us in setting a health project in 1979."

Prayas, a Chittorgarh-based organisation, had an on and off relation with the Oxfam. They stopped taking funds from Oxfam in the early 1980s when they received funds from the government to run a PHC. "They were a little upset. But they bailed us out at a very crucial time when the government stopped our funds for the PHC labelling as anti-national and Naxal. This was because our work on bonded labour had made the government uncomfortable," says Dr Gupta. OGB had given them money to tide over such time till the government released their wages and all the other expenses.

The relationship was revived again in 2003 but through a different affiliate. Between 2003 and 2011, Oxfam Novib supported Prayas in two blocks—Choti Sadri and Badi Sadri—on a project that focused on developing a critical understanding of the social, economic and cultural determinants of health among the community and a system for promoting public action for monitoring health equity and social determinants.

This was a precursor of sorts to Oxfam India's maternal health project rolled out in six states in 2012. The Oxfam Novib project—People's Initiative for Health Security—had a few components that later became a part of the maternal health project such as the emphasis on VHSNCs, groups of adolescent girls and boys, training ASHA and *anganwadi* workers and barefoot auditors.

"It was almost a joint proposal. We had been working on the issue of social determinants of improving maternal health for a long time. So we were made the national secretariat of the project," he says.

Apart from their work on strengthening VHSNCs and encouraging women, adolescent boys and girls to demand for their rights of healthcare, they took up the issue of access to free medicines. In this, they found an ally in Dr Samit Sharma—the newly appointed district collector of Chittorgarh and who later became very popular for his work on free medicines.

Oxfam had in the past on several occasions worked with Prayas on supporting the community to demand and ensure access to health facilities and schemes and therefore, improving their health status. So they became the natural choice of partner to anchor the work and make it more grounded.

"It is a forest till the horizon without any forest guard."

—The concept of Heaven in Gondi religion.

Ensuring the Implementation of Forest Rights Act and Livelihood Options for Forest Dwellers, Especially PVTGs

Chhattisgarh

2011–18

The Recognition of the Forest Rights (Schedules Tribes and the Other Traditional Forest Dwelling Communities) Act, 2006, commonly known as Forest Rights Act (FRA), set out to undo a historical injustice which considered Adivasis and other traditional forest dwellers as encroachers for using and accessing the forest and its resources which they had been cultivating and residing in for generations. The Act made amends by recognising customary rights of forest dwellers, including the right over common areas and the right to manage and sell forest produce. But the impact of the Act has been marred by shoddy implementation, conflicting legislations, attempts to undermine the Act and lack of political will.

The Act finally rolled out in 2008. While Individual Forest Rights (IFR) and Community Rights (CR) were being given (though with some discrepancies), not much had been done regarding the distribution of Community Forest Rights (CFR). A 2010 government report showed poor implementation of the Act especially that of CFR and habitat rights of the Particularly Vulnerable Tribal Groups (PVTG) such as the Pahadi Korwas.

CFRs are extremely important to forest-dwelling communities to move towards decentralised community-based governance and conservation of forests, and recognising their most traditional yet neglected right of grazing. These rights to forest dwellers, the Act asserts, is integral to the survival and sustainability of the forest and biodiversity, most important, from diversion for mining and land acquisition for non-forestry purposes.

As part of Oxfam India's new strategy, it was decided to work in six focus states, that is, Bihar, Jharkhand, Chhattisgarh,

Odisha, Uttar Pradesh and Assam; and among other things, work on the rights of forest dwellers. So the focus shifted from Maharashtra, where it worked in the Vidarbha and Konkan regions on livelihood. Some of these NGOs had worked on Community Forest Rights and proved to be a useful resource for the project in Chhattisgarh.

In Chhattisgarh Oxfam India began from scratch. From identifying partners—the first partner incidentally wasn't working on forest rights but the right to food—training them, organising exposure visits, making gram sabhas functional, forming the forest rights committees, walking them through the process of filing claims and advocating with the state government to ensure that rights were given. These partnerships began in 2012.

Oxfam's efforts bore fruit when Sarguja (Chaupal's villages) became the first district in the state to give away 38 CFR titles. While the recognition of Forest Rights Act (FRA) and distribution of titles have not yet picked up the way the forest dwellers and forest rights activists would have wanted, it has managed to give them confidence and a sense of ownership of the forest and forest resources. They believe that they are the owners of the forests and not the forest department.

Jal, Jangal, Zameen

Oxfam India and Ganga Bhai

On our way to Bule village from Ambikapur, on an April afternoon, Ganga Bhai reminisces of his days when he worked with the Right to Food (RTF) Campaign—the social audits, the *jan sunwais* and the subsequent raids of PDS shops.

"वो हमें naxal से जोड़ते थे। (*They used to think we were naxals*)," he laughs.

He was one of the troublemakers. He had the backing of the likes of Jean Dreze, Aruna Roy, Nikhil Dey and Biraj Patnaik. And those were initial days.

Belonging to the Kanwar tribe, Gangaram Paikra, better known as Ganga Bhai, is an eminent Adivasi rights activist from Sarguja and the president of the Chaupal Gramin Vikas Prashikshan Evam Shodh Sansthan (CVGPESS), also known as just Chaupal. A RTF activist at heart, he ventured into the implementation of FRA in 2011. And this was when Oxfam decided to work on forest rights and livelihoods in Chhattisgarh.

Having met with decent success in forest rights and natural resource management projects in Maharashtra, Oxfam wanted to replicate something similar in Chhattisgarh, their new focus state. But this was new terrain and the team from the Mumbai office began scouting for new partners. One of the most obvious was Ganga Bhai, for various reasons.

"We were looking for organisations working with a rights-based approach and led by a tribal or a Dalit activist. Ganga Bhai was a well-known RTF activist, had a devoted team, shared a good rapport with the district administration and had earned a stature working among the tribals in the district," Anand Shukla had said when we met the day before leaving for Ambikapur. He is the regional manager of Oxfam's Raipur office at present. He was earlier managing the project from the Mumbai office; the Mumbai office was then shifted to Raipur in 2013.

Rebecca David, who was overseeing the economic justice programme in Maharashtra, recalls a field visit to Chaupal's project area in December 2010. "Some of his villages had made conservation efforts in their forests, despite not getting any CFR titles; only a few had received their individual forest rights. For instance, one of the villages had made a road of about 2–3 km to be able to improve their access to the forest. There was zeal and community spirit and we knew that they would be able to take up the work on CFR that we wanted to do."

Rebecca was with Oxfam from 2010 to 2013, after which she moved to the Poorest Areas Civil Society (PACS) programme. Both she and Anand were critical in getting the ball rolling in Chhattisgarh. And they made their presence felt through a huge public hearing on RTF in October 2011.

The state government, in order to weed off ineligible recipients of the PDS, had taken away the cards from a lot of people. As it turned out, many who actually deserved the Antyodaya Anna Yojana (AAY) cards such as widows, disabled and the PVTGs also had their cards taken away. Oxfam and Chaupal collected these testimonies and held a public hearing in March 2011. This was attended, among others, by Biraj (the supreme court commissioner in the RTF case), SC Behar (the former chief secretary of MP and the chief architect of Gram Swaraj in MP) and Sachin Jain (RTF activist).

"This became a huge thing. The SC commissioners issued a letter to the Chhattisgarh government, which started a drive to reinstate the ration cards that were wrongly cancelled. This was a success. The public hearing showed that social movements could bring a change," she adds. We met at her house in Raipur in 2018.

Having made a mark in the state, the next step was to convince NGOs to work on CFR titles. When Oxfam approached Chaupal to work on CFR titles, they were a bit hesitant, said it was too difficult. "We were into movements but winnable movements. The board was okay with working on IFR and especially for the PVTGs. But CFR was new for us and we didn't have the capacity," Ganga Bhai explains the initial reluctance, which was soon overridden by the realisation that it was the need of the hour. They had become Oxfam partners in 2012.

Those at Chaupal were taken on exposure visits to Mendha Lekha, in Maharashtra's Gadchiroli district; this was one of the first two villages in the country to claim CFR title. Simultaneously, Chaupal held meetings with district officials to convince them. "We met the collector and DFO at Sarguja. They understood the need for it and agreed to work with us."

Ganga Bhai tweaked his ways of working. He was quick to realise that he had to work closely with the gram sabha and the panchayat secretaries; the latter was also on the Forest Rights Committee. The panchayat secretaries, incidentally, used to be on his radar when he was fighting to streamline PDS. To win them over, he confesses to turning a blind eye on a couple of occasions. This in fact, made the forest department a little uncomfortable, he says with a chuckle.

Keshav Gurnale of SRISHTI (an NGO based in Gadchiroli district in Maharashtra), regularly visited Chaupal and their villages to walk them through the importance of the CFR titles and handhold them through the process of filing claim. SRISHTI, an Oxfam partner in Maharashtra, was already working on filing claims for their villages.

One of the reasons why NGOs weren't keen on working on CFR or why they weren't being claimed more often was because it was process-heavy, there was a lack of understanding at all levels, and the systems such as the district-level committees were not in place.

Chaupal worked with the Forest Rights Committee to map the forest land, file the claims, get the land independently mapped and approved by the forest department and present it to the Sub-Divisional Level Committee (SDLC). A year later in 2013, Sarguja became the first district in the state to file claims and get it.

The titles were given away with huge fanfare in the presence of the then chief minister Raman Singh but the titles were incomplete and came with riders. While they got grazing and *nistar* rights, and collection of non-timber forest products (NTFPs), they were not given conservation and management rights. The gram sabhas have, nevertheless, formed the CFR management committees and drawn plans for conservation and management of forests.

"Though the forest officials were keen on cooperating, they backed out at the last moment and insisted that we take the case to Raipur. We were suggested by district officials to either take what we were getting or forfeit it entirely." Chaupal took it but decided to continue fighting for it.

And so did Oxfam India. They held state consultations almost every year bringing officials from the forest and tribal ministry, district officials, officials from neighbouring Maharashtra, community leaders and NGOs on the same platform. "Some of the officials said 'Oxfam was becoming revolutionary'," laughs Anand. Backed with testimonies, a lot of allegations and counter-allegations flew thick and fast at these meetings. "The officials must have decided never to do this again with NGOs," smiles Rebecca. The upside of these consultations was that it made a few allies and also built a bridge between officials and the community.

As we negotiate the bad roads out of Ambikapur, Ganga Bhai steers the conversation to his work with the PVTGs. "I was working with Pahadi Korwas and I had made it very clear to Oxfam that I would continue working with them. That was a non-negotiable from my end." Oxfam India had to limit itself to 20 villages, so it selected villages with a lot of forest area. Ganga Bhai made sure that these were villages where the Pahadi Korwas lived!

His concern is that the more privileged tribes such as the Kanwars (to which he belongs), Oraon and Gond will find a way to get their individual titles. "There will be someone in authority from their community to get the work done, but there will be no one for the PVTGs to take up their cause."

Ganga Bhai lobbied for the Pahadi Korwas with the then district collector, Ritu Sain, as well. She turned out to be an ally who assured her support. "The Pahadi Korwas weren't able to give an exact measurement of their land, so we mapped their land. In fact, the collector asked us to train their officials in GPS as well." Chaupal, now trained on GPS mapping, did it for free but with one condition. "We requested the collector to issue an order to her officials to see to it that the Pahadi Korwas get their titles."

Notwithstanding his 'naxal' anecdote, Ganga Bhai over the years built a decent rapport with the district collectors—whether it was R Prasanna at the time of the first CFR claims or Ritu Sen on the issue of Pahadi Korwas'. Not only did Sarguja become the first district in the state to get CFR titles, it got titles for 38 gram sabhas (nearly 20,000 ha) and IFRs for over 1,800 Pahadi Korwa households.

It is not for nothing that he is called *'Pahadi Korwa ka masiah'*!

We finally pull into Bule village in front of a large white hall. "The new Gram Sabha Kendra," he says with a sense of pride.

Making Sense of Gram Sabha

This Gram Sabha Kendra holds a place of pride for both Ganga Bhai and the Bule village. It symbolises the point at which the gram sabha became an institution, for the village community. "Gram sabha simply meant the four meetings held annually. The concept of it being an institution was missing," says Vijendra Aznabi, programme officer at Oxfam's Raipur office.

In fact, an inept gram sabha is very convenient for any government, especially if the forest holds rich prospects for mines, dams and power plants! The Bhakurma Gram Panchayat in Udaipur block, of which Bule is one of the villages, was surveyed for coal mines and River Rend (as Rihand is called in these parts), which flows through the panchayat, for a dam.

An incident changed this outlook. Ganga Bhai recalls an episode when many IFR claims submitted by the village got rejected. "They were made to sign some documents and misguided by the gram sabha." Or rather by the very skeletal structure of gram sabha that existed.

It was this incident that made them realise the role and importance of gram sabha as a local self-governance body. "And when Oxfam started working with Bule village, we began by laying emphasis on the gram sabha. Who else would give the approval for their community claims once they started filing for community forest rights?"

Eventually, the community realised that the gram sabha was required for building roads, for approving work under Mahatma Gandhi National Rural Employment Gurantee Act (MGNREGA) or for implementing the Forest Rights Act. The Gram Sabha Kendra was an assertion of the fact that the village community was taking control of their village governance. The Kendra, different from the Panchayat Bhawan, is usually under the charge of the secretary of the FRC or CFR Management Committee.

"It might just look like a building but the fact is that without this, the gram sabha was weak and mostly non-existent. This hall has given them a place to hold meetings and an office to go to," says Ganga Bhai as we settled down for the meeting.

In fact, for this Kendra, the villagers, after identifying the land, met with their MLA and Congress leaders TS Singh Deo (or 'TS Baba' as he is famously called) with a request to fund it. He partly funded it, the villagers contributed for the rest. It was inaugurated in 2016. After Bule, the neighbouring Sitkalo village, also one of Oxfam's project village, demanded a Gram

Sabha Kendra in their village. In Rajnandgaon, the FRCs and CFR management committees started working from out a deserted school building that the village occupied.

The Gram Sabha Kendra at Bule was a single-storeyed, well ventilated, one hall white building of about 900 square feet; a stack of mahua collected and kept in one corner; a few posters on why the community needs to reclaim their forest was put up on the walls, a few were rolled up waiting to be put up.

In fact, one of the women looks familiar. A few seconds later, one can't help but notice that she is also in the poster in the background, leading women out of a forest. Birulia is one of the five women in the 15-member CFR Management Committee. Though there is participation of women, women leaders, especially in Sarguja, are the missing link. They do come for gram sabha meetings and speak up on issues related to pensions, IFR titles even or NTFP sales. But otherwise, they mostly come and sign. This is something, Ganga Bhai concedes, needs working on.

Anyhow, the meeting began. Few members of the Jungle Bachao Badhao Samiti, the village's renamed CFR Management Committee, are there for the meeting; most of them were away in the field for paddy harvests.

Reclaiming Their Forest, Their Land

For the tribals and other traditional forest dwellers, the forest is their source of sustenance. But it is very difficult to snap out of the mindset that the forest belongs to the forest department and that they are just the caretakers on behalf of the department. The sense that the 'forest is theirs' is gradually beginning to sink in.

So even while they got their titles in 2013, these were incomplete titles with only grazing rights and NTFP collection. They formed the CFR Management Committee only in 2017. In between, they had trainings and workshops, went on exposure visits, understood the FRA, their rights, their power, federated their FRCs, formed the Jungle Bachao Badhao Samiti, resisted the forest department and some untoward encroachers, strengthened their gram sabha and also experimented with a cooperative of sorts.

Bule has a mix of Majhwars, Manjhi, Oraon and the Pahadi Korwas. Though the Pahadi Korwas have received their IFR titles, they are not part of the CFR Management Committee; they live deep in the forest and quite far from the Gram Sabha Kendra making it very difficult for them to participate in these meetings.

As we settle down, Ganga Bhai explains how forest titles are perceived as a *hathyaar* (a weapon). "There is a growing sense among quite a few that they are responsible for conserving and managing the forests. And they are fiercely protective about it. The *dabdaba* of the forest department has reduced." *Sarpanch* Somaru Ram spells out the rules they have drawn regarding grazing, drawing forest lines to prevent forest fires and stopping outsiders—villagers and forest department included—form coming to their forests.

In a recent case, they were protesting after a villager from the Manjhi community bought land from a Pahadi Korwa. The women were at the forefront and they were opposing this sale because the buyer was beginning to fell trees and clear the patch he bought. They have held several meetings with both and the buyer from the Manjhi community refuses it all the time. "We will now write to the ranger and call him for meetings."

A similar case came up in Kardhana in Batauli block. They wanted to stop neighbouring villages from coming to their part of the forest and felling trees. But the catch was that the neighbouring villages had the bank, the post office, the police station and even the market—Kardhana was dependent on them after all. This did get heated up. The district federation intervened; the SDM was brought in. A deal was struck. "They are allowed to come in on Thursday and Saturday and collect dry branches for firewood and some NTFP. But they are not allowed to cut trees," said Rajnath Tirkey. He is the chair of the district FRC Federation and the *sarpanch* of Kardhana for the last 15 years.

Committees impose a fine for felling trees and forest fires. Kardhana went a step ahead. Chaupal requested the FRC in Kardhana, in 2017, to do some plantation in the forest. "To which they said that they don't need more plantation. They were asked a simple question, 'How will you guarantee that the forest is not harmed and no sal trees are cut?'" recalls Vijendra.

And they found a solution. The marriages in these villages use nine slats/poles (to make the *mandap,* a structure under which the marriage ceremony takes place) made of sal; so every time there was a wedding, the relatives would go into the forest and cut a tree. The FRC put a stop to this practice and made it mandatory to reuse the dried slats for all marriages. "We have got them painted and it has to be reused. It is made available to the family for a fee of ₹50 per slat," says Rajnath.

That they are gradually accepting the fact that they own the forest is evident from the big plans that the communities are making. Rajnath's village made big plans for agriculture once they received their titles. They partially dammed and then diverted the water of river Ghungata. This diverted water was channelised to farms by making narrow drains; some of it was also diverted to the homes where the water was used in the kitchen gardens. The village has now diversified—earlier they grew wheat and sugarcane, now they have expanded to paddy, maize, oilseeds and vegetables.

"We have diverted some water towards a patch in the forest which we have prepared to grow climbing vegetables. This is for a simple reason. The vegetables that we will grow on that patch will be for the animals of the forest, whatever will be excess will be brought to the village," he said.

As part of conservation and management of forest, the FRC made a plan on what has to be planted and what not. The FRC opposed the forest department when they wanted to plant eucalyptus as part of their plantation drive. "This would only benefit them. No bird nests in these trees, the leaves are not good for the soil. We couldn't have grown herbs and medicinal plants around them." Rajnath's village wanted fruit trees and bamboo, instead.

Exploring Livelihood Options

The idea of bamboo, to the communities in Sarguja, came during their exposure trip to Mendha Lekha. "The project focussed on livelihood and CFR. When we started, we envisioned that in 5–10 years down the line, they would have MFP and NTFP cooperatives. If Maharashtra could do it with bamboo, why can't we do the same with tendu leaves? This was the dream we had. And it did happen in some places. We pushed this despite the political climate we were in," says Rebecca.

Ganga Bhai had run a cooperative like structure in the 1990s—a group of tribal women who started with agriculture and eventually ventured into catering. He wanted to give NTFPs a shot. Bule experimented with it and were successful, albeit briefly.

"We started by talking about *charota* (NTFP) and niger seeds (oilseeds grown upland and in farms in the forest). This would help them come out of the clutches of contractors and moneylenders," explains Ganga Bhai. There were several SHGs in Bule; they went with the five most active ones. They weren't given a formal cooperative structure yet, that would mean a lot of paperwork and he wanted to see how it would pan out.

In a nutshell, instead of selling directly to the contractors, the village would sell their produce to the SHGs. The SHGs would pay the villagers—for which they got initial funding from the cooperative society—and then sell it when the prices were higher. In the first year, they earned profits and even paid a dividend to the villagers, as well. In fact, the profits encouraged the neighbouring villages to come to these groups to sell their produce to the contractor.

After a good run for over a year, the SHGs started imploding. "The scale was too much for the women. Then the man who was bookkeeping for the SHGs usurped money and ran away. The operations had an impact on the middlemen, who started offering higher rates, almost double, to the forest dwellers—an amount that the women SHGs couldn't match.

They were very good in 2015–16. But had to completely stop in 2017," explains Vijendra.

Rebecca unpacks it further. "The funding was reducing. In Maharashtra, the Mendha Lekha bamboo experiment was successful also because apart from the community and the NGO, the state government backed it."

It might have been an experiment, which didn't take off, but it comes with invaluable experience. More importantly, this episode hasn't dampened spirits. Ganga Bhai says that perhaps they should start with a smaller cooperative, diversify from Mahua and hire a professional for the day-to-day functioning of the cooperative. But funds are shrinking and that is a concern. Vijendra is a little more cautious. The NTFP prices are volatile so that needs to be taken care of.

Somaru *Sarpanch* is more hopeful given his little experiments with selling sal leaves and seeds, tendu, char, charota, amla have given them good returns. They would like to diversify to honey and *dhoop* (sal juice). Rajnath too is thinking in terms of venturing into the bamboo market. And so are others.

Perhaps, this is the time to put their heads together, get back to the drawing board and draw a better livelihood plan!

Building a State Network

"Network *mast hai!* (The network is great!)" pat comes the reply from Ganga Bhai on the question of whether networks and alliances like the Community Forest Rights-Learning and Advocacy (CFR-LA) work.

In 2015, goaded by the Prime Minister, the state government went into overdrive and issued orders to hasten the process of giving claims to the tribals and forest dwellers. Albeit, in blatant violation of the law. This would have flown under the radar, had it not been for a meeting organised by PACS in Raipur where an official from the forest department accidentally spilled the beans during a presentation he was making. The forest rights activists in the meeting cottoned on to it, roped in the CFR-LA which dug into details overnight, petitioned, made a huge hue and cry and finally got the order revoked.

This wouldn't have been possible if a network like CFR-LA wasn't around, he says.

Citing another incident in around 2017, Ganga Bhai recalls how when the state imposed a Mahua trade policy, restricting its trade, the tribals pressed the panic button and started throwing away excess Mahua they had with them. Once again the network picked it up. The government had to retract this policy as well.

Though a knowledge platform like CFR-LA is important for information, knowledge sharing, capacity building and advocacy, he feels that it is too 'national' and not easily accessible to activists like him. For state activists, a more state-specific network was required.

"While it is an excellent knowledge and advocacy platform and serves its purpose for the larger national advocacy, they are unable to take up the very local issues of tribal atrocities and evictions. Also since these are emails and in English, grassroots organisations are unable to access it," Vijendra Aznabi, from Oxfam's Raipur office, voices Ganga Bhai's concerns.

Just like CFR-LA was Oxfam India's (Delhi office) brainchild, the idea of Chhattisgarh Van Adhikar Manch

(CVAM) was born from Oxfam's Raipur office. The idea was to make it inclusive and sustainable by making it a people's movement. The idea was to not limit it to NGOs and their partners and to the Forest Rights Act. The idea was to not have a structured form of a network or make it top-heavy, instead focus on reaching out to as many as possible.

"We have a very active Whatsapp group. So every little detail, for example, of the National Forest Policy reached to the farthest community member. It was put out in Hindi." The network consolidated in 2014–15 and has had a good run since then. "CVAM has earned its identity and it is recognised by officials," Vijendra adds. I was meeting Vijendra and Anand at the Raipur office. This office, though not the secretariat (in the formal sense of the word) holds network meetings, sends out press releases, writes memorandums and provides technical support.

The Oxfam Raipur office is the hub of CVAM!

The CVAM is a very fluid network barring about 12–15 organisations that are regulars. Organisations and community leaders who work on displacement with farmers and women, and on human rights are also a part of this network. The key to the network are community members, that is, the members of the Forest Rights Committee. It was different when Oxfam started working. There was reluctance amongst the villagers to join the committee. Even if their names were there they wouldn't go for meetings.

"In their heads, they equated it with the Joint Forest Management Committee (JFMCs) that had etched very bad memories. Yadavs' and OBCs, who were office bearers for almost 90 per cent of the time, dominated the weaker caste and tribes, destroyed their crops and used the JFMC to settle inter-community disputes and conflicts. It took several meetings and training to convince them that FRC would validate their claims," says Vijendra.

Getting the CFR claims was a boost. But, seeing the process encouraged the committee members to federate at the sub-divisional and later the district level. Some of these FRCs have now converted into CFR management committees and they are all a part of the CVAM.

"I remember one of the FRC members writing to the SDM demanding all the information that was required to file the claims. On another occasion, the district-level federation of Rajnandgaon (comprising 27 villages) sent a letter to the district demanding grants for 61 villages, which received their CFR titles, to 'draw the plan', that is, to purchase stationery, maps. It is one thing to ask for the execution of the plan and quite another to draw the plan," smiles Vijendra.

It is another matter what came of it but the sheer confidence with which they are now taking up issues shows that they have found strength in numbers!

"Freedom is never voluntarily given by the oppressor; it must be demanded by the oppressed."

—Martin Luther King Jr.
Letter from Birmingham Jail
16 April 1963

Networks and Alliances
Gender. Education. Right to Food. Government Policy
2000–19

...And sometimes the oppressed need a voice.

Oxfam's experience has shown that by joining hands with like-minded NGOs and individuals it can be that voice. Historically, Oxfam has worked with and formed networks and alliances. In 1942, the Oxford Committee for Famine Relief was formed by a small group of people who felt anguished about the impact of 'total war' on helpless civilians. Since then, it hasn't shied away from joining hands with others to make an impact on the lives of those who need aid and assistance.

The legacy that started with the many Oxfams working in India such as OGB and Oxfam Novib has continued with Oxfam India. A lot of thought was put into building these network and alliances—they were thematic and cause-based and helped generate momentum for greater advocacy and campaigning. The ways of association might have changed over the years—especially the transition from OGB to OIN—from building networks (with investments in institutional costs) to working with alliances (supporting more on advocacy and campaigning and almost nil institutional cost). Though it moved towards networks and alliances, OIN has continued with its grassroots programmes that are key to evidence-based research to push for campaigning and advocacy through a larger platform.

Over the years, OGB and later OIN brought together networks such as Jumav Manch (on issues related to women empowerment in Jharkhand) that became instrumental to the success of a South Asia Campaign We Can End Violence Against Women, the RTE Forum (on ensuring the implementation of the Right To Education Act), Community Forest Rights-Learning and Advocacy (a knowledge platform for work on Community Forest Rights, one of the most important and yet the most neglected aspect of the Forest Rights Act) and Wada Na Todo Abhiyaan (a national campaign to make government accountable for policies that end poverty, social exclusion and discrimination). These have been documented in the chapters. Others based on a larger idea of network and alliances have been dealt through other stories in the book.

The idea of the book was to document the 10 years of Oxfam India but it would have been incomplete without the mention of Jumav Manch that was formed in 2000. It is important for its design and the paradigm shift it ushered. It showed how programmes, projects and partnerships could be developed, nurtured and tailored to the changing political, and subsequently, social scenarios, and be successful. And two, this was a milestone for Oxfam (in India) where it formed a network of NGOs for grassroots work, campaigning and advocacy, instead of working with individual NGOs.

It wouldn't have been feasible to roll them into one big story so they are dealt as separate sections in this story. The stories give a glimpse of what went into building these networks and alliances, what made them click and the kind of inroads they could make in the political circuits as well as within the communities. It also looks at the model of influencing that Oxfam India is pursuing—that of building knowledge, facilitating research and influencing through networks and coalitions.

Bringing Change, Together

A Network and a Campaign

Jharkhand and Jumav Manch are twins. Well, almost. Both were born only a few days apart in November 2000.

One was the 28th state of India and the other, Jumav Manch (short for, Jharkhand Mahila Vikas Manch) was a network of about 30 organisations that came together to work for women's empowerment and development. One came to life in the colourful lawns of the Raj Bhawan in the new state capital Ranchi, while the other was christened at Hotel Konark a few kilometres away. The timing, however, wasn't a coincidence.

The wheels were set in motion when it had become amply clear that the demand for a separate state was very certainly going to be met. The Jharkhand movement, demanding a separate statehood that began in 1921 was fast approaching the finishing line in 2000, but its problems were far from over. Bihar was riddled with unemployment, lawlessness and lack of development. The new tribal state would get all of this as part of the legacy in addition to complications of its own, that is, exploitation of the Adivasis by the *dikus* or outsiders, the rights on forest resources, and marginalisation and displacement of tribal communities and backward communities for the sake of industries, power plants and mines.

Having worked in Bihar and aware of the political chaos, Chanchal Sinha, OGB's project officer in charge of Bihar (and later Jharkhand) and Shaheen Nilofer, gender officer, kept their ears firmly to the ground. They held meetings with big and small NGOs (within the state as well as neighbouring states), grassroots organisations and activists to understand what the teething problems of the new state were likely to be and what problems needed to be solved. Most of 2000 was spent on meetings and ideation. Three strands of work were identified—*jal, jangal, zameen* and displacement of tribals; marginalisation of Dalits; and status of women.

Oxfam was working on women's development and empowerment and it realised that a new state like Jharkhand would have to start from scratch. New systems would have to be put in place especially to deal with crimes and violence against women and girls, and hence there was immense scope to work on this. OGB was working with gender partners in undivided Bihar but they were small and focused on empowering women through collectives. Advocacy wasn't their core strength. So a network was strategic for advocacy and building new systems.

Jharkhand was formed on 15 November. The very next day, Oxfam called a meeting of nearly 70 NGOs they were in talks with. "These organisations had been a part of the planning process. They had their expertise. Three networks were formed and the organisations picked the network they wanted to be a part of," says Ajay Bhagat of ASHA, a Ranchi based NGO. On 25 November, three networks were born—the Dalit Adhikar Suraksha Manch; Vistapith Mukti Manch; and, Jharkhand Mahila Vikas Manch or Jumav Manch. ASHA joined the Jumav Manch, as did 29 other organisations.

Jumav Manch was going to play a crucial role in the We Can Campaign. But that was still a few years away.

Ajay had registered his organisation a few months before Oxfam formed these networks; he was among nearly 25 NGOs that were formed around this time. "I was a project coordinator in another organisation, which was working closely with Oxfam. Chanchal ji encouraged us to set up our own organisations. Oxfam wanted to support smaller, more grassroots organisations. And here we are today," smiles Ajay. We meet at his office in Bhusur village, on the outskirts of Ranchi. Also present were HI Fatmi of SPARK (Society for Participatory Action, Research and Knowledge) and Manohar Kumar of Jan Sarokar, both members of the Jumav Manch and both sharing the same origins. They like to call themselves the batch of 1999–2000.

The first few years of the network, between 2000 and 2004, were spent in building perspective and capacities, both organisational and individual. And Oxfam played a crucial role. On the one hand, there were exposure visits and gender trainings and, on the other, finance systems and organisational structures were being set up. This network was a mix of older organisations that were working specifically on issues of witchcraft, dowry deaths or child marriage and new organisations such as ASHA, SPARK and Jan Sarokar that were finding their feet so it was essential that they were all on the same page.

A study was conducted to find a common narrative for the network. This bore fruit. "When a network of 25–30 NGOs spoke on women's rights and ending violence against women at the same time in 24 districts, it lent a lot of credence not just to the issue at hand, but also to the organisations involved," says Fatmi. Whether it was sit-ins at Ranchi's Albert Ekka Chowk and Birsa Munda Chowk for women's rights or a postcard campaign demanding panchayat elections in the state, Jumav Manch garnered huge support and credibility and met with a fair share of success.

The State Women's Commission is one such case in point. Jharkhand did not have one until 2006. And Jumav Manch demanded one from the very beginning. "So, on the one hand, we advocated with the government, on the other, we ran a parallel women's commission. The state finally set up the commission in 2006. We shared an excellent rapport with the officer who had been appointed to the commission and we ensured that they had all the help to run properly," says Ajay.

They let me into their little secret—when the newly appointed officer shared with them the tiny logistical issue of finding office space for the commission, Ajay, Fatmi and few others broke into a vacant room in an engineering college in Ranchi and occupied it to provide office space. Such was the camaraderie and commitment to the cause!

In the initial years, up to 2004, the network focussed on building women collectives, which amongst other things were meant to keep a vigil on the incidences of violence against women. But what got them a foothold in the community were the anti-alcohol and de-addiction drives. "This could have been tricky as this would hurt household incomes; liquor was brewed and stocked at homes. But once it was made out to be the villain in the domestic violence narrative, communities went with the collective. This was our first victory," recalls Fatmi. Women-led organisations were encouraged to join the network.

The network was on a roll after that—women came out of their homes, participated in panchayat elections, emerged leaders (in 2011, 112 women won), attended gram sabha meetings, took control of development work (roads, MGNREGA) and involved youth in their monitoring work. Then there was the campaign for bringing the Domestic Violence Act. Jumav Manch went in all guns blazing—postcard campaigns and all. "If others knew that Jumav Manch was going to be there, others who were not part of the network would readily join in. We had a lot of backing. We still do," Ajay says.

The numbers of NGOs in the network might have fallen—from 33 to 17—but it continues to be one of the strongest networks in the state working on violence against women. And the only surviving network of the three formed in 2000. "The reason is simple—everyone is a leader, each one of us has a say. And we are family," chips in Manohar.

The confidence of being able to garner a crowd and run a campaign even today is pretty high. And this comes from their rigorous work during the We Can years. The We Can Campaign ran from 2004 to 2011. They refer to these years as a लहर (wave) and आँधी (storm). It is impossible to miss the enthusiasm in their voice, and the glint in their eyes, as the three talk about the campaign.

"It gave us our first international trip to Sri Lanka and our first passport!" laughs Ajay.

On a more serious note, the We Can Campaign took the gender debate a notch higher. Ajay explains, "It was no longer just about discrimination, it was about domestic violence. It was about drilling in the fact—both within the network and out in the community—that violence wasn't okay; that it wasn't normal for a husband to beat up his wife; and, that it was neither okay to suffer nor inflict violence."

The presence of the network in the state and solid grassroots work made the We Can Campaign a household name. Between 2004 and 2011, it had over 2,00,000 change agents in the state alone. The campaign returned the favour by making the network fundamentals stronger and their outreach wider. The network in Jharkhand, as did all the other partners and networks in other states such as Sanjha Manch in Bihar and Uttarakhand went all out. They reached out to the adolescents in schools and colleges and to youth through village games and fairs. There was a deluge of information to choose from—posters, pamphlets, pledge cards. We Can became the talk of the town. Domestic violence had become the bad guy!

OGB had launched the We Can End All Violence Against Women (We Can) Campaign in 2004. This six-year campaign started in six South Asian countries[1]—Afghanistan,

---

[1] It later extended to Indonesia, the Netherlands and British Columbia in Canada.

Bangladesh, India, Nepal, Pakistan and Sri Lanka. It aimed at making violence against women a visible issue and challenged the deep-set social attitudes that perpetuate discrimination and violence against women. The trigger for the idea was the data of 36 million missing girls in India—a finding that economist Amartya Sen came up with in the 1980s. By the turn of the century, this number touched 50 million.

Oxfam was working on gender-based violence in many states in India as well in South Asia, but Mona Mehta, who has been with OGB for nearly 15 years, explains the rationale behind a campaign, "While grassroots programmes were crucial, a need was felt to reach out to more people. The programmes focussed either on redressal or on women's collective—the former kicked in when the harm was already done and the latter had sustainability issues. Moreover, these were in pockets. There was a need to bring a transformation in the society to end violence against women. Talks of a campaign started making the rounds."

This was in 2000. It would take another four years before the campaign would be flagged off. There were several rounds of discussions and a considerable amount of research looking into how different world movements brought about social change. It all boiled down to changing social behaviour. And Sen's 50 million became the reference point for the outreach.

"Both the concept and the scale were daunting. Back in 2000, or even in 2004, it was very courageous to think about changing social norms in South Asia," she says. But the condition of women in the South Asian countries was such that it was screaming for help—honour killing, child marriage and forced early marriage, abuse and domestic violence.

Unlike the programmes that kept men out of their ambit, the campaign proposed to include them. The key was to get voluntary and sustained participation from men and women, not see men as perpetrators but as change-makers, create individual awareness and personal change, and finally go all out in engaging with the communities.

Those who opted to join the campaign and be change-makers or change agents were encouraged to first recognise, understand and address the acceptance of violence in their own lives, attitudes and behaviour. And then seek to persuade others to do the same. The messaging was simple—violence against women is unacceptable and equal relationships are violence-free. The target was to reach out to 5 million change agents who would reach out to 10 women each.

For a campaign of South Asian proportions—600 organisations from Bangladesh, Nepal, Sri Lanka, India and Pakistan—a lot of out-of-the-box thinking was required. The organisations, which came on board, were largely set in their ways working either on redressal or collectives, so getting them to agree to work on changing social behaviour was tough. Then, there was the issue of having a common voice. Each country was already working on issues that plagued them the most; for example, Nepal was working on human trafficking and Pakistan concentrated on honour killing. It took almost a year of brainstorming and several discussions before domestic violence was decided as the common thread and therefore, the binding theme.

But how does one engage and mobilise people? The outreach target was still daunting. "For Oxfam, this was transformative. Policy changes meant advocacy with government institutes. But this was advocating with the community, mobilising them and challenging social norms." Forming the alliance was the best option and the most sustainable.

The strategy was that the core alliance of organisations, with which Oxfam had a long-standing relationship, would gradually expand to include many more like-minded NGOs, state departments, bilateral agencies, corporate organisations and students.

And, thus was formed the We Can Alliance.

This is where networks such as Jumav Manch played a huge part in making it a 'लहर' and an 'आँधी'!

The Alliance acquired a separate identity from Oxfam. In 2008, along with the formation of the OIN came up the discussion of where the Alliance would sit or how it would continue from thereon. It was decided that instead of being a part of OIN, it would remain autonomous. Mona elaborates on the teething issues, "For instance, for OGB, it was fine to not have visibility and remain in the background. But for an organisation like OIN, which was new and was trying to find its feet, visibility was important. This was a little contradictory to OGB's idea of an alliance, and OIN did try to work around it but was unable to."

From the OIN perspective, Nisha Agrawal, the then CEO says, "OIN was an Indian organisation and we saw ourselves as part of the civil society. We wanted to work with them rather than work like a funding agency. This is perhaps not what the We Can secretariat expected from us."

The We Can Campaign may have ended but even today campaigns such as Enough (ending violence against women campaign) and *Bano Nayi Soch* (social norms campaign) continue to use the spirit of We Can, somewhere. In fact, in the later years, when OIN focused on the PWDVA, this was an offshoot of the We Can Campaign.

What the We Can Alliance did for networks like Jumav Manch was that it gave them a solid grounding in campaign and advocacy and the drive to fight for a common cause. "We might not be working together but all of us have a strong bond till date. We might have shrunk in numbers but even today we can all come together for a common cause without batting an eyelid," says Ajay.

The Alliance may be over, the funds may have shrunk but the enthusiasm is the same as the day they first got together to form Jumav Manch.

Steering the RTE Forum

"Every network has a history of its own. And so did the RTE Forum," Anjela Taneja says as we settle down for a chat at CARE India's office in Noida in April 2018. It had been less than a year that she had joined here, after a three-year international assignment. Within six months, she would be back in Oxfam India heading its Inequality Campaign.

When the RTE Act came into force in 2010, it was at a critical juncture but it also divided the civil society working on education. Some saw it as a historical opportunity to work towards ensuring that the Act was well implemented, while some thought the Act was inadequate. "The Act was fait accompli. So the best-case scenario was to work towards its effective implementation," she says.

To monitor the new Act would require a concerted effort. It would require everyone to come together on one platform. As it turned out, this was the tough part. Between August 2009 (when the bill was passed in the parliament) and April 2010 (when the act came into force), several rounds of discussions were held to iron out differences and build a consensus. Within the larger INGO, there was a lack of clear understanding regarding their stand and position. Those who wanted to hit the ground running felt they were losing the crucial honeymoon period to advocate.

Oxfam India was beginning to take the lead and set the agenda. Anjela cottoned on to it and decided to join Oxfam; she was with Action Aid at that point of time. "Here was an opportunity to set the wheels in motion." As a symbolic gesture, she wanted to resign on 15 August. "But the Internet didn't work that day!"

I am now almost certain that her wry humour was at work for the words 'This publication is copyleft' to find its way in the preliminary pages of the Annual Stocktaking Report of the RTE Forum!

Just around the time she landed the education portfolio in Oxfam India, leadership in the education portfolio changed in other INGOs. The older lot gave way to young blood that were pretty much on the same page—they saw merit in going beyond grassroots work (which was also important) and joining forces for advocacy. There was a need for a network.

But the incessant meetings and discussions within the echo chambers were beginning to seem both endless and pointless. One such meeting in Lucknow, Anjela recalls, was the tipping point. Ambrish Rai, an education activist associated with the Peoples Campaign for Common School System and a regular in these circuits, lost his cool and demanded that action be taken. Led by Oxfam India and supported by NGOs such as Save The Children, CARE, Plan India, CRY and Action Aid, a national network—the RTE Forum was formed in 2010.

Ambarish, a seasoned movements man, became the national convener of the RTE Forum. And the secretariat was placed with the Centre for Social Development. Networks and individuals working on education across the country were mapped. They had to be brought together, it didn't matter that they didn't always agree with each other. It was important that they were all on board.

State networks such as Uttar Pradesh's SCoRE, which predates the RTE Forum and which incidentally was formed with the initiative of Oxfam India's Lucknow office in around 2010, became a part of the RTE Forum. As an aside, SCoRE got the much-needed boost from the national-level Forum and as a state RTE Forum, it has been able to push for stricter implementation of the Act. The good offices of the founding members and enthusiastic officers in the regions played a pivotal role in making the network inclusive and truly pan-Indian. Now the RTE Forum had NGOs and individuals, national and state-level networks, teachers' unions and educationists. Over 10,000 NGOs, civil society organisations and individuals across the country became a part of the RTE Forum!

There were no separate funds allocated for the Forum; the money was routed through the grassroots programmes. For instance, Oxfam India supported Lokmitra in UP for their work on School Management Committees, and Sikshasandhan in Odisha for their work on multilingual education. Meetings, public hearings, reporting and workshops of the Forum were organised through these partner NGOs.

On 1 April 2011, the Forum released its first RTE Stocktaking Report. Anjela's brainchild of sorts, the report provided data-backed evidence on the implementation of the Act in year one and provided a plan of action of sorts for the activism and advocacy for the Forum in the next year. Use of fresh data and numbers mined from media, local information from local NGOs, RTIs and reports like PAISA (Planning, Allocations and Expenditures, Institutions Studies in Accountability Report on utilisation) and ASER (Annual Status of Education Report on learning outcomes) made the report very relevant. Barring DISE, which was a year late, the report had fresh numbers and therefore, a more immediate perspective.

Anjela recalls Nisha being pleasantly surprised at the report launch. "She knew of the network but perhaps hadn't expected the scale. At the launch, members of NAC were floating around while I, one of her programme coordinators, was launching the report. There was no branding. In fact, the backdrop had logos of nearly 30 organisations in the alphabetical order. This put the UN at the end," she chuckles.

Nisha gives complete credit to Anjela for driving the network. Anjela hat-tips the institutional backing which was an enabling factor in the leadership role that Oxfam India assumed. It helped that Oxfam India wasn't invasive. It had just been a couple of years that Oxfam India was registered as an Indian NGO (and not the India office of a foreign NGO) and it had to tread carefully around the civil society lest they were seen jostling for 'funding' space. Although in the case of the RTE Forum, it became clear that Oxfam India was expected to lead from the front. And since there was no funding involved, it wasn't a donor-partner relationship. "We had never broken a network. We weren't even that old," Anjela smiles. Oxfam India did well to bring the civil society together and form the network.

Between 2011 and 2014, the Forum's achievements were exemplary. They went to the Supreme Court to defend the 25 per cent reservation for children in economically weaker sections (EWS) category in private schools. The RTE Forum was up against the private school lobby. In 2012, the top court upheld its constitutional validity. The Forum also sought a ban on all sorts of child labour; in August 2012, the Union Cabinet cleared a proposal to ban all work for children under the age of 14 and restrict non-hazardous work to adolescents between the ages of 14 and 18. Although the members weren't too happy with this as it still didn't ban child labour in households!

The network continues to work effectively, though some fatigue did set in it at some point. And there were some external as well as internal factors at play. Externally, the power at the Centre changed, civil society space began shrinking and the Act seen as Congress legislation became inherently evil for the new regime. However, it isn't entirely a lost cause. "There are still some takers for technical expertise and the network will have to tweak its rules of engagement. It will have to move beyond the 'implement-RTE-Act' attitude. It might be more productive to tell them how to do it," she said.

Internally, Anjela moved to an international network and within a few months, most of the founding members either moved on or moved up. She came back almost after a gap of three years in 2017. For a few months that Anjela was at CARE India, it became the hub of the network.

As she joined back in 2018, Oxfam is once again in the thick of things. The energy that each and everyone, including Ambarish and Anjela, brings to the table has made RTE Forum a force to reckon with.

Backing the Fight Against Hunger Deaths

The Koshish Charitable Trust has a small two-room office on Fraser Road in Patna. But the size of the office cannot be the measure of the work the NGO has done in the past either as the member of the steering committee of Right to Food (RTF)

Campaign in the state or its current endeavour on labour issues. "We are advocating with the state government for Portable Card for Access to Entitlement so that the migrant labourers can get their share of ration in their place of work. This is to ensure their food security," says Rupesh, secretary of Koshish and the state adviser to Supreme Court's commissioners on the RTF case.

Rupesh ji, as he is mostly addressed, is a regular at Oxfam India's regional office in Patna and so our second meeting is scheduled in our office in October 2018. Ranjana Das, the regional officer at Patna had accompanied him to document a starvation death in Rohtas a few months ago and that is perhaps why a meeting was scheduled at the office.

He very kindly complies to my request for a quick chat on his association with Oxfam. "The RTF Campaign had prepared a report on 150 hunger deaths in the state. This was in 2010. Oxfam India supported the network and we were able to release the report at press conferences in three places—Gaya, Araria and Patna," he says.

"The money wasn't much, about ₹10,000, but the impact was huge. It was after this that the Shatabdi Anna Kalash Yojana was started that very year," he adds. Funds were allocated through the Disaster Management Authority; the district had to keep a stock of 10 quintals of grain for any victim of starvation and after providing the grain, it had to ensure that the victim was brought under the RTF scheme. In fact, the recent visit to Rohtas exposed the gaping loopholes in the scheme and its poor implementation.

The RTF Campaign was a decentralised network, which was built on local initiative and voluntary cooperation of individuals and NGOs working on the different aspects of the right to food. The Campaign began with a writ petition submitted to the Supreme Court in April 2001 by People's Union for Civil Liberties, Rajasthan, demanding that the country's gigantic food stocks be used without delay to protect people from hunger and starvation. Apart from NGOs and networks in different states, academicians such as Jean Dreze, Ritika Khera and Dipa Sinha and social activists such as Harsh Mander and Aruna Roy backed the RTF Campaign.

Oxfam India did not nurture the network. In fact, its support was issue-based. For instance, in Odisha, Oxfam supported an NGO called the Right to Food Campaign Odisha (RTF Campaign Odisha) and not the network RTF Campaign. The Odisha NGO was promoting a model of community-based monitoring through village volunteers who were being trained to monitor the implementation of the scheme.

In Bihar, however, Oxfam supported the RTF Campaign with documentation and technical inputs. "This lent huge credence to the campaign in the state." He adds, "The OIN support also meant that gradually other INGOs also began supporting the network. As a result, we came out with a composite report with solid evidence-based research which gave our work a lot of heft."

With this backing of Oxfam and other INGOs, the RTF network in the state was able to push for the first time, social audits on ICDS and MDM. These audits started with Araria and Khagaria. "Later in Motihari as well, as the ICDS director was from there and soon it became mandatory. Until then social audit was conducted and mandated only for MGNREGA," chips in Ritwij, an associate of Rupeshji at Koshish.

Oxfam India supported the network through its different phases—at its peak, when the RTF Campaign held *jan sunwais* or public hearings, and during the slower days with training and district consultations. This continuous support ensured that the network in the state was not just event-based, that is, to report instances of hunger deaths, but issue-based, that is, building a solid base for advocacy and making it a political issue. That the RTF Campaign was able to keep a constant watch and build their programmes on community-based monitoring of the schemes, helped improve PDS distributions and reduce leakages in the system.

With Oxfam standing firmly behind the RTF Campaign and Koshish, wider East India consultations were held with participation from Jharkhand, Bihar, West Bengal, Odisha, Chhattisgarh, Assam and Madhya Pradesh; all laggard states on nutrition and poverty.

Oxfam India's support ended in 2016. "This along with reduced budgetary allocations for social schemes meant that we are not able to keep that kind of pressure on the government and that has impacted the implementation of the Act," says Rupesh. The National Food Security Act, which made the right to food a legal right for the poor, was passed in 2013. He hopes

Oxfam India can once again back them on their endeavour on social security in the state. Our meeting ends.

Joining Forces to Fight Poverty

It was the mid-term appraisal of the 11th five-year plan. Amitabh Behar recalls going in and asking Montek Singh Ahluwalia, the deputy chair of the Planning Commission, 'Who are you to make your own plan and monitor it as well?' "He stopped that meeting and said, 'What do you mean? Who will do it?' And I had said, 'We will do it. The people's campaign, the civil society will do it.'" The year was 2010 and Amitabh was the convener of Wada Na Todo Abhiyaan (WNTA).

At the time of interviewing him for the book, in 2018, he had just joined as the CEO of Oxfam India.

The people's campaign, he refers to, is the WNTA. This is a national coalition of over 3,000 organisations working across states, the Centre for Budgetary and Governance and Accountability (a think tank that worked towards bringing people-centred perspective on policy and budget) and National Social Watch (a network of civil society organisations working on monitoring governance).[2] This coalition or alliance was the group that wanted to hold the government accountable for the promises it made to its people.

In 2007, a picture of an elephant showing 'Common Minimum Programme (CMP) Promised' and a goat showing

[2] https://www.oxfamindia.org/sites/default/files/WP7-Civil-Scty-n-plcy-mkg-in-India.pdf

'CMP Delivered', illustrating the difference in scale, was a huge hit with the media![3]

The nomenclature 'Wada Na Todo Abhiyaan' could have been triggered by a speech Dr Manmohan Singh gave after he was sworn in as the prime minister in 2004. From the Red Fort, he had said, 'that he won't make new promises but will keep the ones made by his predecessor'. The name fit well as this was an attempt to build a citizen's movement to make government accountable.

Reverting to the Planning Commission incident, Amitabh continues, "They took it in the right spirit. And when the 12th Five Year Plan started, they came to us and said, 'Come and design it with us'." And so civil society became a part of the 12th Five Year Plan's planning process. "This was something that would have been unthinkable without the support of Oxfam." This was a huge win for the civil society, which had been trying to make inroads into the policymaking space. They had finally moved from the 'claimed' space to the 'invited' space.

WNTA was an offshoot of an international people's movement—Global Call to Action against Poverty (GCAP)—that was supported by OGB globally. In 2003, Salil Shetty, an activist on poverty and justice and the chief executive of Action Aid had joined as director of the United Nations Millennium Campaign (UNMC). The UNMC was the UN campaign set up to increase awareness and accountability of the Millennium Development Goals across the world. Salil went about the campaign by reaching out to civil society.

[3] http://lib.icimod.org/record/14033/files/5102.pdf

Meanwhile, the idea of GCAP emerged at a meeting of NGOs in Mozambique hosted by Graca Machel in September 2003, an idea, which had the buy-in of civil society activists such as Civicus general secretary, Kumi Naidoo.

United Kingdom groups had just finished working on Make Poverty History Campaign; GCAP was next in line! That is when OGB came in. So with the likes of Salil and Kumi on board, GCAP became the world's largest civil society movement calling for an end to poverty and inequality. It involved millions of people in mass protests and had some significant successes in changing policies and promises on aid, trade and development and in articulating the voices of poor and marginalised people. The traction was immense; the campaign was a success.

Salil suggested national chapters of GCAP and that is how it came to India in 2004. WNTA emerged from the consensus among human rights activists and social action groups who were part of the World Social Forum 2004 (Mumbai).[4] The network was, therefore, replicated in India. There was a buy-in from all INGOs such as Action Aid, Oxfam and Christian Aid and the local civil society so there was no effort required or time wasted in forming the network. OGB was supporting it globally, but when it convened meetings in India, the question posed by the Indian civil society back then was 'How can you let a national campaign be run by a foreign NGO?' The first year was tepid, verging on a debacle.

OGB, which had been working in India for many years with grassroots organisations and individuals, had no qualms

[4] http://wadanatodo.net/index.html

about letting the Indian civil society take lead. It was after this that Amitabh and Jagadananda (mentor and co-founder of the Centre for Youth and Social Development in Bhubaneswar) became co-chairs. "OGB continued its support," Amitabh remembers.

OGB supported from 2004 to 2014; Oxfam India was formed in 2008. The funding supported setting up a Secretariat comprising five people and an office space. "They had said that we should find the campaign money from wherever, 'but we will give you the secretariat'. This was crucial support—about ₹25 lakh—without which the campaign would not have taken off."

B Muralidharan, Oxfam's South Asia advisor (Millennium Development Goals) from 2005 to 2007, was a massive support to the network. He coined the 'Nine is Mine' Campaign led by children across the country—this was one of the shining examples of WNTA's mass mobilisation. The 'nine' refers to the 6 per cent of GDP on education plus the 3 per cent on health that children claimed as their right. The campaign launched on 16 October 2006 in Delhi and had over 4,500 children participate from ten states.

Muralidharan on behalf of Oxfam was on the steering committee from the very first year. "He brought in a lot of stability. He played an organisational role and was chipping in with every small detail whether it was hiring people or putting out adverts or going to the media using Oxfam's resources." In 2008, Muralidharan moved on to become the advisor to UN Resident Coordinators office.

WNTA worked on three strategies—research and analysis of the performance of the government (for example, civil society reviews of CMP looking at gender and caste issues), mass mobilisation (for example, People's Summit Against Poverty with nearly 12,000 people) and advocacy (with legislators and the people's manifesto prior to elections). And they did well. "With a small amount of ₹25 lakh we were able to make a huge impact. We were recognised as Wada Na Todo Abhiyaan and not GCAP India by the time the SDGs came along. We anchored the civil society inputs of the 12th Five Year Plan. These were massive wins," says Amitabh.

At these times of shrinking civil society space, he feels such networks that question the accountability of the government should have a lot of backing. And hence he feels that perhaps Oxfam ending its support, after 2014, may have been a rational decision but not a very wise one. "WNTA as a campaign always respected the INGOs for their value of providing us with global exposure. They were valued as partners and not just as donors."

Though he is on the other side now, his passion for the network is still palpable. He feels that Oxfam India can still pick up the strings, build on its own legacy and be the influencer it hopes to become. Perhaps it will!

Building a Knowledge Platform

In April 2015, Prime Minister Narendra Modi pulled up eight 'laggard states' for the poor implementation of the FRA. He set a deadline for the states to get into a 'campaign mode' and implement the Act. This set the proverbial cat among the pigeons. What followed was a blatant violation of the Act.

A case in point was the Chhattisgarh government's letter (dated 27 July 2015) asking gram sabhas to issue statements that all FRA claims had been cleared and no eligible claimants remained. These certificates were to be issued by 15 August, when gram sabha meetings were scheduled across the state. But by 13 August, the state government had to retract, thanks to a rap on the knuckle by the Ministry of Tribal Affairs (MOTA) and pressure from forest rights networks.

One of the networks was CFR-LA. A network that could be said to be Oxfam India's brainchild. There were other networks working on the rights of forest communities across the country and in different states. But what triggered Oxfam to initiate another platform was the slow progress in recognising the Community Forest Rights of the forest dwellers.

In 2010, a report by the joint committee of MOTA and Ministry Of Environment and Forest and Climate Change (MOEFCC) recommended that Community Rights, CFRs and Habitat rights for PVTGs required special attention. Though the Scheduled Tribes and Other Traditional Forest Dwellers (Recognition of Forest Rights) Act (known as the FRA) was passed in 2006, the rules for the implementation of the Act were notified on 1 January 2008.

These rights were very critical for forest dwellers to access the entire commons. "This would be a game-changer for the 1,75,000 villages dependent on forests for their livelihoods," explains Sharmistha Bose of the economic justice team. Around the time she joined Oxfam in 2011, the idea of a network or a platform was beginning to take shape. It was around the same time that Oxfam India's first strategy was being drafted and a decision was taken to work with others to ensure that the rights of the forest dwellers were recognised.

Vanita Suneja who was leading the team, back then, shared her idea with activists such as Ashish Kothari of Kalpavriksha (one of the oldest development and conservation NGOs). Ashish was a member of the joint monitoring committee on FRA. But there wasn't much clarity yet. However, Vanita, with a background of having worked on joint forest management and through networks, was certain that this was the way forward.

Then came the March 2011 national consultation at Bhubaneswar; this was organised by NGOs such as Kalpavriksha, Vasundhara and several other grassroots organisations. Deliberations were made on Community Rights, Community Forest Rights, implementation of the Act and the role of the government and civil society. In fact, when CFR-LA was formed, the NGOs leading the process were Oxfam, Kalpavriksha and Vasundhara. Vasundhara, an Odisha-based NGO had worked for nearly two decades on conserving and managing community forests in the state.

"A major outcome was that the grassroots felt a need for collective and community action on CFR. Also, CFR is diverse due to the different ecologies, so the process of mapping them, claiming the rights and then the conservation and management of forests would also be unique. This would require a different kind of focus. The national consultation's recommendation was to set such a process where learning and advocacy can be brought on the same platform," remembers Tushar Dash of Vasundhara.

Based on the recommendations of the national consultation, a meeting was held in December 2011 at the Indian Social Institute in Delhi, to chalk out the strategy for the recommendations. A meeting of the leading forest rights group was held and CFR-LA was given a shape. "There were several groups that were already working but what was missing was a process of collective advocacy and learning process. There was a need to support the larger forest rights groups in advocacy and evidence building," Tushar explains during a Skype call.

There was a discussion on whether the collective should be a network or a platform or an alliance. A knowledge platform was decided upon. "The platform couldn't just have three NGOs leading the process. So the platform would be made inclusive by leveraging the strengths of the other NGOs and groups," says Sharmistha. In fact, since it was a platform and not a formal network, the participation was pretty fluid. There was on and off participation from even those groups who thought that political activism was the need of the day and not a knowledge platform.

The mandate of the group was fourfold and it proved itself on all four counts. One, since the application of CFR was process-heavy, stress was laid on building the capacities of groups applying for these rights; GIS training was given in order to map the commons for applying for CFR. Two, collect and disseminate knowledge and information; an e-group was formed which has over the years served as a useful platform to collate and share information, seek answers and even mobilise. Three, evidence-based advocacy; without this, the Chhattisgarh government would have ridden roughshod over the FRA rules. And, finally, as a round-up of the year to understand the status of implementation of CFR, prepare an annual report and hold a national consultation to decide the future course of action.

In fact, the way the platform has lent support to grassroots has only increased its currency. State consultations were a regular feature and this meant that state networks and even those grassroots organisations that are unable to connect with the platform otherwise have the opportunity to discuss their issues and share their successes.

"If there was a problem regarding filing for titles or understanding the rules, CFR-LA always managed to find a solution. So people saw something fruitful coming out of it and appreciated it," says Sharmistha.

Over the years, the leadership in CFR-LA has become more decentralised; Oxfam has assumed a back seat. Roles and responsibilities are assigned to different NGOs and individuals for sub-groups on national advocacy and research, capacity building and gender issues. For instance, the group on gender issues led by Soma Kishore Parthasarathy—a known feminist, researcher, policy analyst and support person to community-based institution-building initiatives—reflects the commitment of the platform to focus exclusively on women forest dwellers, on their rights, their participation in the forest rights committees, and their role in the conservation and management of forests and women's land rights.

Though in the initial years, OIN was leading the process—at state-level meetings in its focus states—it was never in the forefront. It was clear from the very beginning that in order for the network to find traction in the civil society it had to be seen as an independent network and not an Oxfam network.

"These agencies have believed in the democratisation of forest rights and always been around to extend support," Tushar speaks of NGOs such as Oxfam and Action Aid. Alluding to the shrinking civil society space and the general apathy of the government towards recognising rights of the tribals and other traditional forest dwellers, he calls for more support from these big NGOs.

Funding definitely reduced, a fact we acknowledge. Although in the last few years, CFR-LA did get a fresh lease of life with organisations such as Rights and Resource Initiative (RRI), TISS and Ashoka Trust for Research in Ecology and the Environment (ATREE) bringing in their resources—both as knowledge partners and as funders.

In the last eight years, the implementation of the FRA hasn't panned out the way it was expected to, so there still remains a lot of scope for CFR-LA. Within, Oxfam feels the need to be able to figure out a way to reach out to the farthest of grassroots organisations and support them. On the outside, there is a point of view that believes that Oxfam needs to do a little more. "There is a continuum of work in conservation, management and governance. However, what is missing is the support to community groups." Tushar speaks of the various village-level groups or federations for the conservation and management of forests, run by women and youth that need to be supported.

As we begin to wrap up our Skype call, he slips in a word of advice, "For Oxfam, there is a need to understand the larger perspective of resource rights. CFR-LA is just one network, there are several other networks around us and they need to be assimilated and respected for the sheer fact that these networks have been around for a long time. They have to be more outward-looking."

Oxfam does acknowledge the work of other networks, especially the state networks, and in the last few years has sought collaboration with national networks such as Mines, Minerals and People, BIRSA and Centre for Policy Research-Namati Environmental Justice Programme to work on strategies for advocacy on Free Prior Informed Consent on issues of land and environment.

The fact that expectations are high from Oxfam is a reflection of the faith that other organisations have in Oxfam. This is a win and a very good space to be in!

About the Author

Savvy Soumya Misra started working on the book almost two years ago because she believed that stories of Suresho, Chitamma, Birsa and many more needed to be heard.

She also believes that the work civil society and non-government organisations do never really reaches the general reader because it is lost in the jargon of economic and social theories. These are stories of people and the attempt is to tell these stories in a lucid manner. This is her attempt at reaching out to readers like herself!

A former journalist, the trade helped her break down the complex web of information into smaller, relatable stories. Before joining Oxfam India in 2014, she has worked at the *All India Radio*, *The Telegraph*, *CNN-IBN*, and *Down to Earth* magazine. She found her calling in rural reporting while working at *Down To Earth*, where she travelled extensively. The transition to the development sector thus appeared natural.

At Oxfam India, for the most part, she has been with the Research team, documenting its work. It's been a few months now that she has joined the public engagement team.

The author is a huge fan of the 90's Bollywood music, is crazy about lamps, loves food, and is an occasional knitter.